DYNAMITE COVER LETTERS

Books by Drs. Ron and Caryl Krannich

The Almanac of American Government Jobs and Careers
The Almanac of International Jobs and Careers
Best Jobs For the 1990s and Into the 20th Century
Careering and Re-Careering For the 1990s
The Complete Guide to International Jobs and Careers
The Complete Guide to Public Employment
Discover the Right Job For You!
Dynamite Answers to Interview Questions
Dynamite Cover Letters
Dynamite Resumes
The Educator's Guide to Alternative Jobs and Careers
Find a Federal Job Fast!
High Impact Resumes and Letters
Interview For Success
Jobs For People Who Love Travel
Mayors and Managers
Moving Out of Education
Moving Out of Government
Network Your Way to Job and Career Success
The Politics of Family Planning Policy
Re-Careering in Turbulent Times
Right SF-171 Writer
Salary Success
Shopping and Traveling in Exotic Asia
Shopping and Traveling in Exotic Hong Kong
Shopping and Traveling in Exotic Indonesia
Shopping and Traveling in Exotic Singapore and Malaysia
Shopping and Traveling in Exotic Thailand
Shopping and Traveling the Exotic Philippines
Shopping in Exciting Australia and Papua New Guinea
Shopping in Exotic Places
Shopping the Exotic South Pacific

DYNAMITE COVER LETTERS

Ronald L. Krannich, Ph.D.
Caryl Rae Krannich, Ph.D.

IMPACT PUBLICATIONS
Woodbridge, VA

Dynamite Cover Letters

Library of Congress Cataloging-in-Publication Data

Krannich, Ronald L.
    Dynamite Cover Letters / Ronald L. Krannich, Caryl Rae Krannich.
      p. cm.
    Includes bibliographical references and index.
    ISBN 0-942710-53-3: $9.95.
      1. Job hunting. 2. Cover letters. I. Krannich, Caryl Rae. II. Title.
HF5382.7.K693   1992   91-30091
650.14—dc20   CIP

For information on distribution or quantity discount rates, call (703/361-7300), FAX (703/335-9486), or write to: Sales Department, IMPACT PUBLICATIONS, 4580 Sunshine Court, Woodbridge, VA 22192. Distributed to the trade by National Book Network, 4720 Boston Way, Suite A, Lanham, MD 20706, Tel. 301/459-8696.

CONTENTS

PREFACE

Getting strangers to notice your interests, skills, and qualifications and then take action leading to job offers is what the job search is all about. In every job search activity—be it writing resumes, telephoning for job leads, networking, or interviewing for a job—you must repeatedly make good first impressions so that employers decide to invest more time in your candidacy. One of the most important activities you must learn to do well is writing powerful cover letters and other types of job search letters.

The art of good letter writing is a skill few people possess or use to their advantage. Indeed, many job seekers put their worst foot forward when they write cover letters. They forget it's their cover letter—not their resume—that gets read first by employers. Considering letters as relatively unimportant in comparison to other job search activities, they often generate dull, boring, and deadly documents that do anything but grab the attention of readers and persuade them to invest more time with them on the telephone or in a face-to-face interview. Instead, their letters kill both their resume and their candidacy. This should not happen to you.

This book is all about paper power—getting it, building it, and using it. It's designed to put more power into your paper and greater energy into your job search. We want you to create your own dynamite letters that will lead to improved job search success. As you will quickly discover, this is not your typical book on cover letters. Most such books are primarily filled with scattered writing tips or examples of so-called "outstanding" letters. Our focus is on both **understanding and action** centered around an important **process** aimed at getting employers to **respond to you in positive ways**.

We begin with the role of cover letters in the overall job search process and then focus on the key principles for creating effective cover letters. We do so by examining every stage of the letter writing process, from organizing and writing internal letter elements to producing, distributing, and following-up each letter for maximum impact. Self-evaluation plays an important role throughout this process.

Effective letters involve much more than demonstrating good writing style on pretty paper. At the very least, your letters must be intelligently produced and distributed in reference to the specific needs of your audience. Most important of all, they must be followed-up with the critical telephone call. Neglect any one of these letter writing stages and you will effectively kill your chances of moving employers to respond to you in positive ways. You will produce paper, but your paper will lack power.

We wish you well as you initiate your first contacts with potential employers and other individuals for job information, advice, and referrals. Whatever you do, make sure your paper has power. If you correctly organize, produce, distribute, and follow-up your letters, you will acquire the power to move yourself into the offices of employers!

Ronald L. Krannich
Caryl Rae Krannich

Chapter One

THE POWER
OF PAPER

This book is all about power—increasing your ability to get others to respond to you in positive ways. You have within you the power to shape your future. You can instantly communicate to strangers that you are a professional, competent, thoughtful, and likeable individual. You can get others to stand up and take notice of your qualifications. You can get more employers to invite you to job interviews. And you can open more doors to job and career success.

But you must first take the time and make the effort to clearly communicate your qualifications to employers. You must let employers know you are a serious and desirable candidate. Begin by focusing your attention on the needs of your audience and paying particular attention to the details of powerful communications. That power often begins on paper in the form of dynamite cover letters.

YOU ARE WHAT YOU WRITE

How and what you write tells potential employers a great deal about your professionalism, competence, and personality. Being busy people,

1

employers will make quick judgments about you based upon limited information you present to them. Within only a few seconds, your written message motivates them to either select you in or take you out of consideration for a job interview. Neglect the importance of a dynamite cover letter accompanying your resume, or other types of job search letters, and you neglect one of the most important elements in a successful job search.

The art of good letter writing is more important than ever in today's busy world where many different forms and channels of communication must compete for limited attention. When you initially meet strangers through the written word, you essentially are what you write. Readers of your letters draw certain conclusions about your professionalism, competence, and personality based on both the form and content of your written message. If, for example, you write poorly organized and constructed letters, employers will conclude you are probably a disorganized individual. If you make grammatical, spelling, or punctuation errors, you tell employers you are probably a careless person who is likely to make errors on the job. If you type your letter on cheap paper, use a typewriter that produces unattractive print, or mass produce your letter on a copy machine, you communicate a lack of class. If you fail to accurately address an employer by his or her proper name, title, and address, you communicate other negative messages—you don't take them seriously and you are probably inconsiderate. In the end, employers do not want to be bothered with such types of individuals. They don't want to talk with them nor see them. They definitely have no interest in putting them on their payroll!

COVER LETTERS DO COUNT

Finding employment in today's job market poses numerous challenges for individuals who seek quality jobs that lead to good salaries, career advancement, and job security. The whole job finding process requires a certain level of organization and communication skills aimed at identifying, contacting, and communicating your qualifications to potential employers. If you want to make this process best work for you, you must do more than just mail resumes and letters in response to job vacancy announcements.

To be most successful in finding employment, you need to develop a plan of action that involves these seven distinct yet interrelated job search steps:

1. Assess your skills

2. Develop a job/career objective

3. Conduct research on employers and organizations

4. Write resumes and letters

5. Network for information, advice, and referrals

6. Interview for jobs

7. Negotiate salary and terms of employment

As illustrated on page 4, each of these steps involves important communication skills involving you and others. Assessing your skills, for example, requires conducting a systematic assessment of what you do well and enjoy doing—your strengths or motivated abilities and skills (MAS) that become translated into your "qualifications" for employers. Conducting research on employers and organizations requires the use of investigative skills commonly associated with library research. Networking and interviewing primarily involve the use of conversational skills—small talk and structured question/answer dialogues—by telephone and in face-to-face encounters.

But it is the critical resume and letter writing step that becomes the major communication challenge for most job seekers. Without strong writing skills, your job search is likely to founder. Indeed, your ability to write dynamite cover letters and resumes largely determines how quickly you will transform your job search from the investigative stage (research) to employer contact stages (networking, interviewing, salary negotiations). Your writing skills become the key element in moving your job search from the investigative stage to the final job offer stage.

Most employers want to first see you on paper before meeting you in person. In the job search, paper is the great equalizer—you along with many

JOB SEARCH STEPS

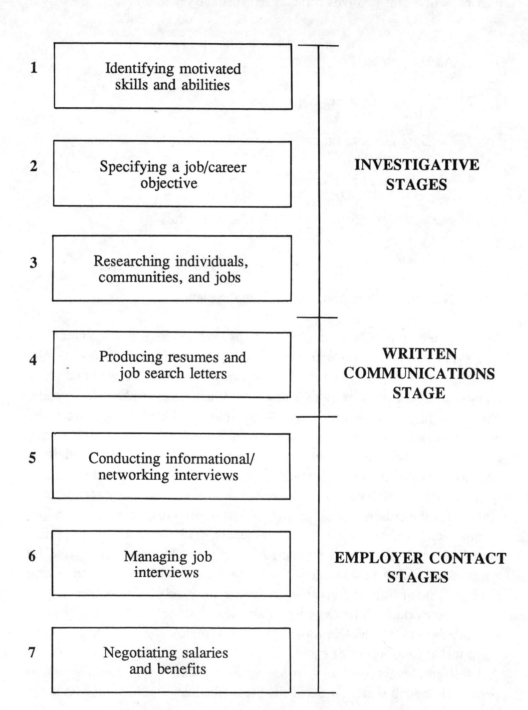

1	Identifying motivated skills and abilities	
2	Specifying a job/career objective	**INVESTIGATIVE STAGES**
3	Researching individuals, communities, and jobs	
4	Producing resumes and job search letters	**WRITTEN COMMUNICATIONS STAGE**
5	Conducting informational/ networking interviews	
6	Managing job interviews	**EMPLOYER CONTACT STAGES**
7	Negotiating salaries and benefits	

others must pass the written test **before** you can be considered for the face-to-face oral test. Whether you like it or not, you must put your professionalism, competence, and personality in writing before you can be taken seriously for a job interview. Thus, your writing activities may well become the most critical transformation step in your job search. Your writing skills are your ticket to job interviews that lead to job offers and employment.

> ### *You must put your professionalism, competence, and personality in writing <u>before</u> you can be taken seriously for a job interview.*

For some reason job search writing skills usually receive little attention beyond the perfunctory *"you must write a resume and cover letter"* advisory. They also get dismissed as unimportant in a society that supposedly places its greatest value on telecommunicating and interpersonal skills. Indeed, during the past two decades many career advisors have emphasized networking as the key to getting a job; writing resumes and letters are relatively unimportant job search skills. Some even advise job seekers to dispense with cover letters and resumes altogether and, instead, rely on cold calling telephone techniques and "showing up" networking techniques. Others still accept the importance of resumes but downplay the role of cover letters by advising job seekers to put handwritten notes at the top of their resume in lieu of sending cover letters to potential employers:

"Here's my resume in response to your vacancy announcement."

But let's get serious about what's being communicated here. In a job search aimed at business and professional circles, proper procedures and communication etiquette do count. While expedient, such handwritten notes on resumes communicate the wrong messages—you don't take the job nor the employer seriously. Handwritten notes are most appropriately written to subordinates by superiors or to relatives, friends, and acquaintances. And few people have attractive handwriting to complement what should be an attractively printed resume.

When conducting a serious job search, it is simply inappropriate to treat potential employers as subordinates, relatives, friends, or acquaintances by scribbling a handwritten note on your resume. They deserve and expect better from strangers who are attempting to persuade them to do something they ordinarily would not do—invite you to a job interview. Being in a position with the power to hire, they expect to receive properly constructed written communications appropriate for their position and indicative of your level of professionalism.

It is inappropriate to treat potential employers as subordinates, relatives, friends, or acquaintances by scribbling handwritten notes.

Like much of today's career advice, the scribbled personal note advisory neglects the important role **both** written and interpersonal communication play in the overall job search. Being preoccupied with the "latest technique" for achieving job search success, such advisors fail to see the forest for the trees. They have yet to appreciate the critical **transformation role** written communications play in the larger seven-step job search process.

While some individuals do get interviews by scribbling notes at the top of their resume, you can do much better if you take the time and effort to craft a thoughtful cover letter. That letter should focus on the employer's needs. It should reinforce the professionalism, competence, and personality which you are ostensibly demonstrating in your attached resume. Without an effective cover letter, your resume, as well as the remaining steps in your job search, may have limited impact on potential employers.

IMPROVE YOUR EFFECTIVENESS

Just how effective are you in opening the doors of potential employers? Let's begin by identifying your level of job search information, skills, and strategies as well as those you need to develop and improve. You can do this by completing the following "job search competencies" exercise:

INSTRUCTIONS: Respond to each statement by circling which number at the right best represents your situation.

SCALE:
     1 = strongly agree
     2 = agree
     3 = maybe, not certain
     4 = disagree
     5 = strongly disagree

1. I know what motivates me to excel at work.   1 2 3 4 5

2. I can identify my strongest abilities and skills.   1 2 3 4 5

3. I have at least seven major achievements that clarify a pattern of interests and abilities that are relevant to my job and career.   1 2 3 4 5

4. I know what I both like and dislike in work.   1 2 3 4 5

5. I know what I want to do during the next 10 years.   1 2 3 4 5

6. I have a well defined career objective that focuses my job search on particular organizations and employers.   1 2 3 4 5

7. I know what skills I can offer employers in different occupations outside education.   1 2 3 4 5

8. I know what skills employers most seek in candidates.   1 2 3 4 5

9. I can clearly explain to employers what I do well and enjoy doing.   1 2 3 4 5

10. I can specify why employers should hire me.   1 2 3 4 5

11. I can gain support of family and friends
    for making a job or career change.   1 2 3 4 5

12. I can find 10 to 20 hours a week to
    conduct a part-time job search.   1 2 3 4 5

13. I have the financial ability to sustain
    a three-month job search.   1 2 3 4 5

14. I can conduct library and interview research
    on different occupations, employers,
    organizations, and communities.   1 2 3 4 5

15. I can write different types of effective
    resumes and job search/thank-you letters.   1 2 3 4 5

16. I can produce and distribute resumes and
    letters to the right people.   1 2 3 4 5

17. I can list my major accomplishments in
    action terms.   1 2 3 4 5

18. I can identify and target employees I
    want to interview.   1 2 3 4 5

19. I can develop a job referral network.   1 2 3 4 5

20. I can persuade others to join in forming
    a job search support group.   1 2 3 4 5

21. I can prospect for job leads.   1 2 3 4 5

22. I can use the telephone to develop prospects
    and get referrals and interviews.   1 2 3 4 5

23. I can plan and implement an effective
    direct-mail job search campaign.   1 2 3 4 5

24. I can generate one job interview for every
    10 job search contacts I make.   1 2 3 4 5

25. I can follow-up on job interviews.   1 2 3 4 5

26. I can negotiate a salary 10-20% above
    what an employer initially offers.   1 2 3 4 5

27. I can persuade an employer to renegotiate
    my salary after six months on the job.   1 2 3 4 5

28. I can create a position for myself
    in an organization.   1 2 3 4 5

                                    TOTAL   _____

You can calculate your overall job search effectiveness by adding the numbers you circled for a composite score. If your total is more than 75 points, you need to work on developing your job search skills. How you scored each item will indicate to what degree you need to work on improving specific job search skills. If your score is under 50 points, you are well on your way toward job search success. In either case, this book should help you better focus your job search around the critical writing skills necessary for communicating your qualifications to employers. Other books can assist you with many other important aspects of your job search.

---

*The whole purpose of a job search is
to be taken seriously by strangers
who have the power to hire you.*

GET TAKEN SERIOUSLY BY EMPLOYERS

The whole purpose of a job search is to get taken seriously by strangers who have the power to hire you. Your goal is to both discover and land a job you really want. You do this by locating potential employers and then persuading them to talk to you by telephone and in person about your interests and qualifications.

Being a stranger to most employers, you initially communicate your interests and qualifications on paper in the form of cover letters and resumes. How well you construct these documents will largely determine whether or not you will proceed to the next stage—the job interview.

The major weakness of job seekers is their inability to keep focused on their purpose. Engaging in a great deal of wishful thinking, they fail to organize their job search in a purposeful manner. They do silly things, ask dumb questions, and generally waste a great deal of time and money on needless activities. They frustrate themselves by going down the same deadend roads. Worst of all, they turn off employers with poor communication.

The major weakness of job seekers is their inability to keep focused on their purpose.

The average job seeker often wanders aimlessly in the job market, as if finding a job were an ancient form of alchemy. Preoccupied with job search **techniques**, they lack an overall **purpose and strategy** that would give meaning and direction to discrete job search activities. They often engage in random and time consuming activities that have little or no payoff. Participating in a highly ego-involved activity, they quickly loose sight of what's really important to conducting a successful job search—responding to the needs of employers. Not surprisingly, they aren't taken seriously by employers because they don't take themselves and the job search serious enough to organize their activities around key communication behaviors that persuade employers to invite them to job interviews. This should not happen to you.

The following pages are designed to increase your power to get taken seriously by employers. Individual chapters show you how to create and distribute dynamite cover letters that command the attention of employers. Individual chapters:

- Explore numerous myths about cover letters.

- Outline effective writing principles.

- Discuss different types of cover letters.

- Examine the structure of letters.

- Outline effective production and distribution strategies.

- Show how to best implement and follow-up job search letters.

- Present several examples of cover letters and related job search letters.

THE PRODUCT AND THE PROCESS

While it is tempting to fill the following pages with numerous examples of model job search letters, such an approach would probably prove ineffective for you. An approach that focuses solely on examples of the **product** implies you should "creatively plagiarize" the examples in order to create effective cover letters. More importantly, it neglects the whole **process** that is key to job search success—knowing how to organize, produce, distribute, and follow-up each product.

The following chapters focus on the four stages of the letter writing process. Like the job search in general, effective letter writing involves four distinct sequential stages, as illustrated on page 12:

1. Organizing

2. Producing

3. Distributing

4. Following-up

EFFECTIVE LETTER WRITING PROCESS

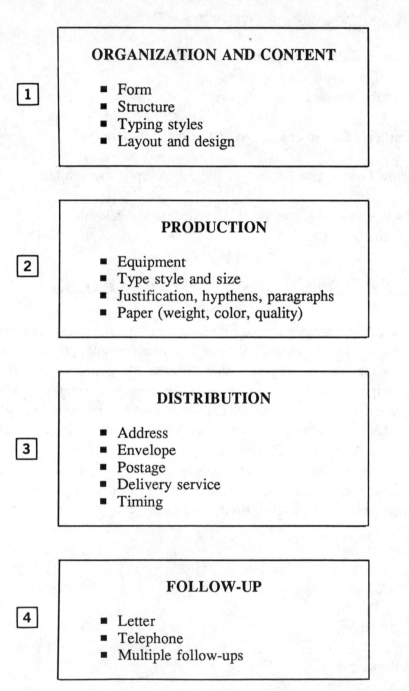

1

ORGANIZATION AND CONTENT

- Form
- Structure
- Typing styles
- Layout and design

2

PRODUCTION

- Equipment
- Type style and size
- Justification, hypthens, paragraphs
- Paper (weight, color, quality)

3

DISTRIBUTION

- Address
- Envelope
- Postage
- Delivery service
- Timing

4

FOLLOW-UP

- Letter
- Telephone
- Multiple follow-ups

Each stage involves certain principles that contribute to the overall effectiveness of your letters. To be most effective, your letters must adhere to the principles that define each stage. The letter writing stages, in turn, are related to other important job search steps, such as networking and interviewing, which have their own principles for effectiveness.

Therefore, the examples in this book are presented to illustrate important **principles** involved in these letter writing stages. They should not we used as examples to be copied or edited. As you will discover in the following pages, it is extremely important that you create your own letters that express the "unique you" rather than communicate "canned" messages to potential employers.

In the end, our goal is to improve your communication effectiveness in the job search. On completing this book, you should be able to write dynamite cover letters that result in many more invitations to job interviews.

DO WHAT'S EXPECTED AND PRODUCES RESULTS

Based on experience, we assume most employers do indeed expect to receive a well crafted cover letter accompanying an equally well crafted resume. We proceed on the assumption that cover letters are just as important as resumes in the job search. In some cases the cover letter may be even more important than the accompanying resume. In fact, many employers report that dynamite cover letters really catch their attention; they persuade them to interview individuals they ordinarily would not have interviewed had they just read their resume.

The old interview adage that *"you never have a second chance to make a good first impression"* is equally valid for the cover letter. For it is usually the cover letter rather than your telephone voice or appearance that first introduces you to a prospective employer. Your cover letter tells them who you are and why an employer should want to spend their valuable time meeting you in person. It enables you to express your personality and style—two important ingredients that are difficult to demonstrate in standard resume formats. It invites the reader to focus attention on your key qualifications in relation to the employer's needs. It enables you to set an agenda for further exploring your interests and qualifications with employers.

Once you see the importance and function of well crafted cover letters, you will never again let your resume reach potential employers without first prefacing it with a dynamite cover letter. For in the end, it may well be your cover letter, rather than your accompanying resume, that is responsible for getting you invited to the job interview!

CHOOSE THE RIGHT RESOURCES

This book is primarily concerned with communicating your qualifications in writing to employers who, in turn, will be sufficiently motivated to invite you to a face-to-face job interview. Several of our other books deal with the key steps in the job search process as illustrated on page 4: *Careering and Re-Careering for the 1990s, Discover the Right Job For You!, High Impact Resumes and Letters, Dynamite Resumes, Interview For Success, Dynamite Answers To Interview Questions, Network Your Way To Job and Career Success*, and *Salary Success*. Others examine specific career fields, including government hiring processes, public employment strategies, the federal application form, and the special case of educators: *The Complete Guide to Public Employment, Find a Federal Job Fast!, The Almanac of American Government Jobs and Careers, The Right SF-171 Writer*, and *The Educator's Guide to Alternative Jobs and Careers*. If your interests include the international employment arena, we have three books that can assist you: *The Complete Guide to International Jobs and Careers, The Almanac of International Jobs and Careers*, and *Jobs for People Who Love Travel*. For job alternatives, see our *Best Jobs for the 1990s and Into the 21st Century* and *Jobs and Careers With Nonprofit Organizations*. These and many other job search books are available directly from Impact Publications. For your convenience, you can order them by completing the form at the end of this book or by acquiring a copy of the publisher's catalog.

If you wish to acquire a copy of the most comprehensive career catalog available today—*"Jobs and Careers for the 1990s"*—which lists over 1,000 annotated job and career resources, write to:

IMPACT PUBLICATIONS
ATTN: Free Job/Career Catalog
4580 Sunshine Court
Woodbridge, VA 22192

They will send you a free copy upon request. This catalog contains almost every important career and job finding resource available today, including many titles that are difficult, if not impossible, to find in bookstores and libraries. You will find everything from self-assessment books to books on resume writing, interviewing, government and international jobs, military, women, minorities, students, and entrepreneurs as well as videos and computer software programs. This is an excellent resource for keeping in touch with the major resources that can assist you with every stage of your job search as well as with your future career development plans.

DISCOVER YOUR POWER

Whatever you do, make sure you acquire, use, and taste the fruits of job search power. You should go into the job search equipped with the necessary knowledge and skills to be most effective in communicating your qualifications to employers. As you will quickly discover, the job market is not a place to engage in wishful thinking. It's at times impersonal, frequently ego deflating, and often unforgiving of errors. It requires clear thinking, strong organization, and effective strategies for making the right moves with employers. Above all, it rewards individuals who follow-through in implementing each job search step with enthusiasm and dogged persistence.

May you soon discover this power!

Chapter Two

MYTHS AND REALITIES

Conducting an effective job search requires a clear understanding of the job market and how to use effective job search strategies and techniques. Unfortunately, many individuals approach the job market with numerous myths about how it operates as well as misconceptions concerning the most effective methods for achieving success. Many of these myths relate to the role of cover letters and resumes in the job search.

Let's examine several myths that are likely to prevent you from taking effective action in today's job market. These myths, along with corresponding realities, outline a set of important **principles** for best communicating your qualifications to potential employers. They illustrate important points for organizing each step of your job search.

THE JOB SEARCH

MYTH 1:   **Anyone can find a job; all you need to know is how to find a job.**

REALITY: This "form versus substance" myth is often associated with career counselors who were raised on popular career planning exhortations of the 1970s and 1980s that stressed the importance of having positive attitudes and self-esteem, setting goals, dressing for success, and using interpersonal strategies for finding jobs. While such approaches may work well in an industrial society with low unemployment, they constitute myths in a post-industrial, high-tech society which requires employees to demonstrate both **intelligence and concrete work skills** as well as a **willingness to relocate** to new communities offering greater job opportunities. For example, many of today's unemployed are highly skilled in the old technology of the industrial society, but they live and own homes in economically depressed communities. These people lack the necessary **skills and mobility** required for getting jobs in high-tech, growth communities. Knowing job search skills alone will not help these people. Indeed, such advice and knowledge will most likely frustrate such highly motivated and immobile individuals who possess skills appropriate for old technology.

The job market is highly decentralized, fragmented, and chaotic.

MYTH 2:   **The best way to find a job is to respond to classified ads, use employment agencies, and submit applications to personnel offices.**

REALITY: Except for certain types of organizations, such as government, these formal application procedures are not the most effective ways of finding jobs. Such approaches assume the presence of an organized, coherent, and centralized job market—but no such thing exists. The job market is highly decentralized, fragmented, and chaotic. Classified ads, employment agencies, and personnel offices tend to list low paying yet highly competitive jobs. Most of the best jobs—high level, excellent pay, least competitive—are neither listed nor advertised; they are usually found through word-of-mouth. Your most fruitful strategy will be to conduct research and informational interviews on what career counselors call the "hidden job market".

MYTH 3: **Few jobs are available for me in today's competitive job market.**

REALITY: This may be true if you lack marketable skills and insist on applying for jobs listed in newspapers, employment agencies, or personnel offices. Competition in the advertised job market usually is high, especially for jobs requiring few skills. Numerous jobs with little competition are available on the hidden job market. Jobs requiring advanced technical skills often go begging. Little competition may occur during periods of high unemployment, because many people quit job hunting after a few disappointing weeks of working the advertised job market.

MYTH 4: **I know how to find a job, but opportunities are not available for me.**

REALITY: Most people don't know how to find a job, some lack marketable job skills, and they fail to clearly communicate their qualifications to employers. They continue to use ineffective job search methods. Opportunities are readily available for individuals who understand the structure and operation of the job market, have appropriate work-content skills, use job search methods designed for the hidden job market, and are skilled in communicating their qualifications to employers.

---

*If you can define employers'
needs as your skills,
you might end up in
the driver's seat!*

MYTH 5: **Employers are in the driver's seat; they have the upper-hand with applicants.**

REALITY: Most often no one is in the driver's seat. Not knowing what they want, many employers make poor hiring decisions. They frequently let applicants define their hiring needs as the applicant's strengths and capabilities. If you, too, can define employers' needs as your skills, you might end up in the driver's seat!

MYTH 6: **Employers hire the best qualified candidates. Without a great deal of experience and numerous qualifications, I don't have a chance.**

REALITY: Employers hire people for all kinds of reasons. Most rank experience and qualifications third or fourth in their pecking order of hiring criteria. Employers seldom hire the best qualified candidate, because "qualifications" are difficult to define and measure. Employers normally seek people with the following characteristics: competent, intelligent, honest, and likeable. "Likeability" tends to be an overall concern of employers. Employers want **value** for their money. Therefore, you must communicate to employers in writing, over the telephone, and in person that you are such an individual. You must overcome employers' objections to any lack of experience or qualifications. But never volunteer your weaknesses. The best qualified person is the one who knows how to get the job—convinces employers that he or she is the **most** desirable for the job.

If you go after a growth field, you will try to fit into a job rather than find a job fit for you.

MYTH 7:   **It is best to go into a growing field where jobs are plentiful.**

REALITY: Be careful in following the masses into today's so-called hot "in" fields. People who primarily pursue occupations for money, status, position, or perceived future job growth (objective opportunities) rather than for compatibility with their interests and skills (the right "fit") may be in for many career disappointments. First, many of today's glamorous go-go growth fields can quickly experience no-growth as well as major cutbacks—such as aerospace engineering, nuclear energy, architecture, real estate, and defense contracting—when the economy shifts into a recessionary mode or industries experience serious challenges. Second, by the time you acquire the necessary skills for entry into these occupations, you may experience the recurring "disappearing job" phenomenon: too many people did the same thing you did and consequently glut the job market about the time you are ready to enter the job market. Many students completing MBA and law degrees, for example, are the latest casualties of such a job market. Third, since many people leave no-growth fields, new opportunities may arise for you in these fields. Fourth, if you go after a growth field, you will try to fit into a job rather than find a job fit for you. If you know what you do well and enjoy doing and what additional training you may need, you should look for a job or career conducive to your particular mix of skills, interests, and motivations. In the long-run you will be much happier and more productive finding a job fit for you.

MYTH 8:   **People over 40 have difficulty finding a good job.**

REALITY: Yes, if they apply for youth and entry-level jobs. Age should be an insignificant barrier to employment if you conduct a well organized job search and are prepared to handle this potential negative with employers. Age should be a positive and must be communicated as such. After all, employers want experience, maturity, and stability. People over 40 generally possess these qualities. As the population ages and birth rates decline, older individuals should have a much easier time changing jobs and careers.

MYTH 9:   **I must be aggressive in order to find a job.**

REALITY: Many aggressive people also tend to be offensive and obnoxious people. Try being purposeful, persistent, and pleasant in all your job search activities. Such behavior is well received by potential employers.

MYTH 10:   I should not change jobs and careers more than once or twice. Job-changers are discriminated against in hiring.

REALITY: While this may have been generally true 30 years ago, it is no longer true today. America is a skills-based society: individuals market their skills to organizations in exchange for money and position. Furthermore, since most organizations are small businesses with limited advancement opportunities, careers quickly plateau for most people. For them, the only way up is to get out and into another organization. Therefore, the best way to advance careers in a society of small businesses is to change jobs. Job-changing is okay as long as such changes demonstrate career advancement and one isn't changing jobs every few months. Most individuals entering the job market today will undergo several career and job changes regardless of their initial desire for a one-job, one-career life plan.

MYTH 11:   People get ahead by working hard and putting in long hours.

REALITY: Success patterns differ. Many people who are honest, work hard, and put in long hours also get fired, have ulcers, and die young. Some people get ahead even though they are dishonest and lazy. Others simply have good luck or a helpful patron. Moderation in both work and play will probably get you just as far as the extremes. There are other ways to become successful in addition to hard work and long hours.

MYTH 12:   I should not try to use contacts or connections to get a job. I should apply through the front door like everyone else. If I'm the best qualified, I'll get the job.

REALITY: While you may wish to stand in line for tickets, bank deposits, and loans—because you have no clout with the front office—standing in line for a job is dumb. Every employer has a front door as well as a back door. Try using the back door if you can. It works in many cases.

COVER LETTERS

Several additional myths and realities directly relate to cover letters in the job search. Most are communication myths that fail to appreciate the importance of **consistently projecting a professional image** at all stages of a job search. Among the most important myths are the following:

MYTH 13: **Resumes and networking are more important to getting a job than cover letters.**

REALITY: We really don't know what actions produce the most important results for getting a job in any specific individual case. While resumes and networking are important, so too are well crafted cover letters and telephone and face-to-face interviews. Many employers report that impressive cover letters are often more important than resumes in making decisions to interview candidates.

MYTH 14: **The purpose of a cover letters is to introduce your resume to an employer.**

REALITY: A cover letter should be much more than mere cover for a resume. Indeed, it may be a misnomer to call these letters "cover letters." It's best to think of these letters as "interview generating" communications. The purpose of a cover letter should be to get the employer to **take action** on your resume. Consequently, the whole structure of your cover letter should focus on persuading the employer to invite you for a job interview.

The purpose of a cover letter should be to get the employer to take action on your resume.

MYTH 15:   **A cover letter should be only one paragraph in length.**

REALITY: Cover letters should say something about you to the employer. If you can say everything in one short paragraph, fine. While you should try to keep you letter short and to the point, don't limit it to a few lines. Remember what you are trying to do—get the employer to take action in reference to your interests and qualifications as partially outlined in your resume. A well constructed cover letter should be organized like advertising copy:

- catch the reader's attention
- persuade the reader about you or your product
- convince the reader with more evidence
- move the reader to acquire your service or product

Since you need to accomplish a great deal in your letter, this letter will probably run three paragraphs and be confined to one page.

MYTH 16:   **It's okay to send your resume to an employer without an accompanying cover letter.**

REALITY: Only if you want the employer to think his or her position and employment opportunity are not important. This myth is propagated by those who believe employers are too busy to read but not too busy to be pestered by telephone calls and networkers who invite themselves to interviews. Employers initially prefer succinct written communications. It enables them to screen candidates in and out for the next stage of the hiring process—a telephone screening interview. Sending a resume without a cover letter is like going to a job interview barefoot—your application is incomplete and your resume is not being properly communicated for taking action. Cover letters should always accompany resumes that are sent through the mail. They help position your interests and qualifications in relation to the employer's needs as well as indicate what action will be taken next. Above all, they give employers signals of your personality, style, and likeability—important elements in the hiring decision.

Sending a resume without a cover letter is like going to a job interview barefoot.

MYTH 17: **Your cover letter should be addressed to the Director of Personnel or "To Whom It May Concern."**

REALITY: Your cover letter should be addressed to the person responsible for making the hiring decision, which most likely is not the Director of Personnel. Individuals in personnel are normally responsible for announcing vacancies, processing applications, and managing day-to-day personnel matters. What hiring they do is primarily confined to positions within their own unit or deal with lower level support positions that service many operating units. Hiring decisions for most positions are usually made in the operating units rather than in personnel. Always address your letter to a specific person—by name and position—and address them as Mr., Mrs., or Ms. If you don't have a name, call the organization and ask to whom you should address your communications.

Always address your letter to a specific person—by name and position.

MYTH 18:   **Sending a general cover letter and resume to hundreds of employers will increase my chances of getting a job.**

REALITY: Such a non-focused shotgun approach will initially give you a false sense of making progress with your job search because it involves a major expenditure of time and money. But it will most likely increase your level of frustration when you receive few replies and numerous rejections. This approach is nothing more than playing a game of probability where your probabilities are extremely low—a 2 percent response rate would be considered excellent! It's always best to target your resume on specific jobs, organizations, and individuals. A general "To Whom It May Concern" cover letter is destined for the circular files. It indicates you did not take the time to learn about the organization nor the employer's needs. Such random behavior indicates you are not a thoughtful and serious person. Worst still, you appear desperate for a job. How many employers are eager to hire such people?

MYTH 19: **Handwritten cover letters have a greater impact on employers than typewritten cover letters.**

REALITY: Handwritten cover letters are inappropriate as are scribbled notes on or attached to a resume. They are **too** personal and look unprofessional when applying for a job. If you are a professional, you want to demonstrate that you can present yourself to others in the most professional manner possible. Confine your handwriting activities to your signature only. The letter should be typed on a good quality machine—preferably a letter quality printer.

Confine your handwriting activities to your signature only.

MYTH 20: **Your cover letter should summarize your resume, highlight your major strengths, and invite the employer to call you on the telephone for an interview.**

REALITY: Such a cover letter would be unnecessarily redundant, long, and probably boring. Remember, the goal of your cover letter is to answer the key question facing the employer you wish to interview with: *"Why should I invite this person to an interview and perhaps hire her or him?"* Your answers should be immediately evident—preferably in the first paragraph—short, and to the point.

Never volunteer salary information in writing. . . . you negotiate salary after receiving a job offer.

MYTH 21: **Include your salary history and expectations in your cover letter as well as your references.**

REALITY: Never volunteer salary information in writing nor so early in the application process; answers to this question should come near the end of the job interview, when you negotiate salary **after** receiving a job offer. Only include it if the employer specifically requests that your salary history and expectations be included in writing. And when you do, avoid stating a specific salary figure. State "negotiable" or give a **salary range** which should accurately reflect the value of both the position and you. Salary is something that should be **negotiated** at the very end of your job interview. The same principle applies to references. Volunteer your references only upon request, which is often during the interview. Never include them in your cover letter nor on your resume. If you are specifically asked to supply a list of references, do so, but make sure you have contacted the individuals named as your references and briefed them about your job search and this specific position. They should be prepared for an expected phone call from the prospective employer.

MYTH 22: **Always end your letter with an indication that you expect to hear from the employer: "I look forward to hearing from you."**

REALITY: What do you expect will happen when you close your letter in this manner? Probably nothing. While this is a polite and acceptable way of closing such a letter, it is a rather empty statement of hope—not one of action. Remember, you always want **action** to result from your written communication. Any type of action—positive or negative—should help you move on to the next stage of your job search with this or other potential employers. This standard closing is likely to result in no action on the part of the employer who is by definition a busy person. It's better to indicate that **you** will take initiative in contacting the employer in response to your letter and resume. End your letter with an action statement like this one:

> I'll give you a call Thursday afternoon to answer any questions you may have regarding my interests and qualifications.

Such an action statement, in effect, invites you to a telephone interview—the first step to getting a face-to-face job interview. While some employers may avoid your telephone call, at least you will get some action in reference to your letter and resume. If, for example, you call on Thursday afternoon and the employer is not available to take your call, leave a message that you called in reference to your letter. Chances are the employer is expecting your call and will remember you because you are taking this initiative. In some cases, the employer will tell you frankly that you are no longer under consideration. While disappointing, this rejection has a positive side—it clarifies your status so you no longer need to waste your time nor engage in wishful thinking about the status of your application with this employer. Go on to others who may prove more responsive. In other cases, your phone call may result in getting a face-to-face interview early on in the application process with this employer. Taking action in this manner will at least give you useful information that will bring your application nearer to closure. But make sure you call at the time you say you will call. If the employer expects your call on Thursday afternoon and you forget to do so, you prematurely communicate a negative message to the employer—you lack follow-through. Always do what you say you will do and in a timely fashion.

MYTH 23:   **Sign your full name.**

REALITY: What's in a name? A lot. Particular names generate certain positive and negative images amongst employers who are screening strangers for interviews. While most people are content with the name they inherited, others should seriously consider doing something about their name, especially if it is a real negative to their career. Whether you use just your first and last name or include a middle initial depends on your own professional style. In general, the use of a full first name and middle initial tends to communicate a more formal and professional style; it tends to create greater distance between you and the employer. A shortened first name (Bill rather than William or Jenny rather than Jennifer) tends to communicate a more informal style and greater social openness. If you have an unusual name that may distract from your qualifications, such as Kitty Kat, Flagler Finch, or Foxy Trot, consider doing something about it—a formal name change may be in order if it appears your name is a real negative to your career! We too often come across unusual and sometimes hilarious names that prevent individuals from being taken seriously by employers. While your parents may have had fun naming you as a cute baby, life is a more serious business. Whatever you do, try to communicate your particular style in your name, knowing full well employers are looking for serious people.

MYTH 24:   **Sign your letter in black ink.**

REALITY: Again, your signature should indicate your professional style. Black ink is okay, but blue looks better in contrast to black type. It's best to use a fountain pen rather than a ballpoint pen for signing your name. Fountain pen ink communicates more class and indicates a certain professional style that is desired by many employers.

> *Fountain pen ink communicates more class and indicates a certain professional style.*

MYTH 25:   **It's best to produce your cover letter and other job search letters on a typewriter.**

REALITY: Try to keep the type style of your cover letter the same as your resume. Ideally, produce both your cover letter and resume on a word processor using the same printer. Avoid dot matrix printers which look unprofessional and indicate computer generated mass mailings. If you use a desktop publishing program that allows you to choose different type styles for a laser printer, choose Times Roman, Palatino, New Century, ITC

Bookman, or a similar standard type style; avoid Helvetica or an italicized script which are difficult to read. Use nothing less than a letter quality printer. If you use a typewriter, make sure it produces top quality type and is error free—do not erase, use white-out, or apply chalk correcting tape to fix typing errors. Avoid machines that produce amateurish looking or messy type; the type should look neat, clean, and sharp. If you lack in-house capabilities to produce such quality documents, contact someone who does. Many people specialize in producing quality documents at reasonable rates. Do not short-change your job search by producing sloppy and amateurish looking cover letters and resumes.

MYTH 26: **Your cover letter should be produced on ivory or off-white paper.**

REALITY: While paper colors do make a difference in communicating professional styles, there is nothing magical about ivory or off-white paper. As more and more people use this color, the off-white color has lost its effectiveness. Try a light grey or basic white. Indeed, white paper gives a nice bright look to what has become essentially a dull colored process. If you are applying for a creative position, you may want to use more daring colors to better express your creative style and personality.

MYTH 27: **The quality of the paper is not important as long as you type your letter neatly and choose a proper paper color.**

REALITY: Paper quality expressed in terms of weight and texture does make a difference. It, too, communicates something about your professional style and personality. Stay with a 20 to 50 pound bond paper that has the look and feel of a professional document. You achieve the proper look and feel by using 100% cotton fiber or "rag content" paper. Avoid very thin or extremely thick and coarse papers.

MYTH 28:   **Use printed personalized stationery with your name, address, and phone number printed across the top.**

REALITY: While printed personalized stationery looks nice, it's not necessary to go to such an extreme to impress employers. It may be a negative to some employers who think you may be a bit extravagant. It's quite acceptable to produce your letter in a standard blank piece of quality paper; type your return address at the top where it should normally go depending on the letter style you choose.

MYTH 29:   **Sending your cover letter and resume by special next-day delivery services—Express Mail, UPS Next Day Air, Federal Express, or courier service—will increase your chances of getting an interview.**

REALITY: This may be another case of overkill that primarily demonstrates your extravagance in using expensive delivery arrangements rather than result in having a positive impact on the employer's decision-making. While these services will get your cover letter and resume quickly in the hands of the employer, they may not make much of a difference. After all, employers are not prepared to make their decisions on the day your mailing arrives. It's fine to send your communications by first-class mail.

MYTH 30:   **It's best to have machine imprinted postage applied to the envelope rather than use stamps.**

REALITY: We're not sure which type of postage works best. To be on a safe side, use a stamp rather than machine imprinted postage. A stamp—preferably an attractive commemorative stamp—looks nice and is more personal than machine imprinted postage. In fact, many people report better responses to letters mailed with stamps. If you use machine imprinted postage, an employer may think you are abusing your present employer's postage machine. Under no circumstances should you send your letters by bulk mail—stamp, machine imprinted, or indicia. Such mailings communicate two negatives—you are engaged in mass mailings and thus not serious about this employer, and you are cheap. The same holds true for affixing mailing labels to envelopes. All information on the front of an envelope should be typed. Mailing labels are impersonal and communicate "junk mail" and laziness. You may have rented a mailing list consisting of numerous employers!

MYTH 31: **It's best to send your cover letter and resume in a matching No. 10 business envelope.**

REALITY: A No. 10 business envelope requires you to fold your cover letter and resume at least twice. At the receiving end, it requires the employer to unfold it twice and then try to keep it flat in a pile of other similarly folded documents. A non-folded cover letter and resume stands out better in a pile of partly folded documents. We recommend sending your 8 x 11½ cover letter and resume in a 9 x 12 white envelope. Try to find a good quality envelope in this size. Stamp, handwrite, or affix a label that says "First Class" or "Priority" one inch above the left hand corner of the address.

MYTH 32: **Follow-up your cover letter with a copy of the original letter accompanied by a handwritten note in the upper right hand corner inquiring about the status of your application.**

REALITY: This approach lacks class. Always try to follow-up with a telephone call. You should have indicated in the final paragraph of your letter that you would make this call at a specific time. But don't expect to make direct contact with your first phone call. If your first telephone follow-up call fails to put you in contact with the employer, make another three to seven calls until you make direct contact. Keep your cool if your calls aren't returned—many people simply don't return their calls. If after seven calls you still can't get through, write a follow-up letter inquiring about the status of your application and mention your continuing interest in the position. But do not just send another copy of your letter.

While conducting your job search, you will encounter many of these and other myths and realities about how to best communicate your qualifications to employers. Several people will give you advice. While much of this advice will be useful, a great deal of it will be useless and misleading. You should be skeptical of well-meaning individuals who most likely will reiterate the same myths. You should be particularly leery of those who try to **sell** you their advice.

Always remember you are entering a relatively disorganized and chaotic job market where you can find numerous job opportunities. Your task is to organize the chaos around your skills and interests. You must convince prospective employers that they will like you more than other "qualified" candidates. A well crafted cover letter that is properly produced, distributed, and followed up will play a key role in communicating your qualifications to employers.

Chapter Three

JOB SEARCH LETTERS

Written communications should play an important role throughout your job search. Not only do you introduce yourself to prospective employers by writing resumes and cover letters, you should also communicate with employers by producing several other types of job search letters.

The most important job search letters are cover, approach, thank-you, and resume letters. Each of these letters can be subdivided into additional types of letters. Let's survey these letters before we examine the details of writing and distributing cover letters.

COVER LETTERS

The cover letter is a special type of job search letter. By definition it always accompanies a resume and is more or less targeted toward potential employers.

Employers regularly receive two types of cover letters—targeted and broadcast. Each letter provides cover for an enclosed resume.

Targeted Cover Letter

The targeted cover letter is the most commonly written job search letter. It is addressed to a specific person and in reference to a position which may or may not be vacant. It may be written in response to a classified ad or vacancy announcement or in reference to a job lead received from a referral.

A targeted cover letter should be specific and oriented toward the needs of the employer. The content of this letter should reflect as much knowledge of the employer and the position as possible. The writer should emphasize his or her skills that appear most compatible with the needs of the employer and the requirements of the position. It should tell the employer why he or she should take time to talk with you by telephone or meet you in person to further discuss your qualifications. It should communicate both professional and personal qualities about you—you are a competent **and** likeable individual.

Always try to **address this letter to a specific person**, by name and title. A proper salutation should begin with Mr., Mrs., or Ms. If you are unclear whether you are writing to a male or female, because of the unisex nature of the first name or the use of initials only—Darrell Smith or L. C. Williams—use "Mr." or the full name—"Dear Darrell Smith" or "Dear L. C. Williams". Women should always be addressed as "Ms.", unless you know for certain that "Mrs." or "Miss" is the appropriate and preferred salutation. However, many classified ads and vacancy announcements only include an address. Some may appear to be blind ads with limited information on the employer—P.O. Box 7999, Culver City, CA. If you are unable to determine to whom to address your letter, use one of two preferred choices:

1. "Dear Sir or Madam" or "Dear Sir/Madam". This is the formal, neutral, and most acceptable way of addressing an anonymous reader.

2. Eliminate this perfunctory salutation altogether and go directly from the return address to the first paragraph, leaving three spaces between the two sections. We prefer this "open" style since it directs your letter to the organization in the same manner in which the anonymous classified ad or vacancy

announcement was addressed. Your opening sentence will indicate to whom the letter goes.

Whatever your choices, please do not address the individual as "Dear Gentleperson", "Dear Gentlepeople", "Dear Person", "Dear Sir", "Dear Future Employer", "Dear Friend", "Dear Company", "Dear Personnel Department", or "To Whom It May Concern". Employers are neither gentlepeople nor friends; a "sir" often turns out to be a female; you should not be so presumptuous to imply you'll be working there soon; and a company or department is not a person. Such salutations do nothing to elevate your status in the eyes of a potential employer. Several are negatives; most verge on being dumb! It's perfectly acceptable to follow the time-honored rule of *"When in doubt, leave it out."*

The targeted cover letter is designed to directly **connect** you to the needs of the employer. It is normally divided into three distinct paragraphs. In response to a classified ad or vacancy announcement, for example, the first paragraph of this letter should connect you to the advertised position by way of introduction. For openers, make your first sentence connect you directly to the employer's advertising efforts:

> I learned about your sales and marketing position in today's Record-Courier.

The remaining sentences should connect your skills and goals to the position and organization:

> I learned about your sales and marketing position in today's Record-Courier. I have seven years of progressive sales and marketing experience in pharmaceuticals, involving $3.5 million in annual sales. I'm interested in taking on new challenges with a highly respected and innovative pharmaceutical firm that values team performance and wishes to explore new markets.

Such an opening paragraph is short, to the point, grabs attention, and avoids the canned language and droning character of so many boring and pointless cover letters received by hiring personnel. Our letter emphasizes four important points:

- Where and when you learned about the position—you make a logical and legitimate connection to the employer. Also, employers like to know where candidates learn about the vacancy in order to determine the effectiveness of their advertising campaigns.

- You have specific skills and experience directly related to the employer's needs.

- You are interested in this position because you want to progress in your career rather than because of need (you're unemployed) or greed (you want more money). Your purpose is both employer- and career-centered rather than self-centered.

- Your style and tone is professional, personal, positive, upbeat, and value neutral. Most important, you appear "likeable." You avoid making canned, self-serving, or flattering statements about yourself and the employer. The reader is probably impressed so far with your skills, interests, and knowledge of his or her firm. The reader's initial response is to learn more about you by reading the rest of the letter as well as reviewing the enclosed resume.

If you send a cover letter and resume in response to a referral, the only change in reference to our first original targeted cover letter (page 38) involves the first sentence. In this case you may or may not be responding to a specific position vacancy. An employer may be surveying existing talent to see what's available to the organization for possible personnel expansion. This is an example of how an employer may hire someone without ever advertising a vacancy—behavior in the so-called "hidden job market." He or she may want to let the market determine whether or not the organization is interested in adding new personnel. In this cover letter, the emphasis again is on making a legitimate connection to the employer. The tone is more personal:

Jane Parsons, who spoke with you on Friday about by interests, suggested I contact you about my sales and marketing experience. She said you wished to see my resume.

I have seven years of progressive sales and marketing experience in pharmaceuticals, involving $3.5 million in annual sales. I'm interested in taking on new challenges with a highly respected and innovative pharmaceutical firm that values team performance and wishes to explore new markets.

This is the best type of referral you can receive—an intermediary already introduced you to a potential employer who is requesting your resume. She has already legitimized your candidacy and screened your qualifications based on her own judgment and personal relationship with the employer. If she is highly respected by the employer for her judgment on personnel matters—or better still if the employer "owes her a favor"—you have an important foot in the door. At this point you need to reinforce her judgment with a well-crafted cover letter and resume immediately followed up with a phone call. In this case you need not mention a specific position being advertised since it may not actually be advertised. Include only the name of your referral as well as refer to those interests and skills you already know are compatible with the employer's interests. Keep in mind that the opening sentence—personal reference to your referral—is the most important element in this letter.

The remaining paragraphs in this type of targeted letter will follow the same form used for other kinds of cover letters—emphasize your relevant experience and skills, which are summarized in your resume, and call for action on your resume. We'll examine these other paragraphs in subsequent chapters.

Broadcast Cover Letter

Broadcast cover letters are the ultimate exercise in delivering job search junk mail to employers. These letters are produced by job search dreamers. These are basically form letters sent to hundreds, perhaps thousands, of employers in the hope of being "discovered" by someone in need of your particular qualifications and experience. This is a favorite marketing method used by job search firms that charge individuals to help them find a job. It is their single most important indicator—however ineffective—that they are performing for their clients. The broadcast cover letter and resume proves to their clients that they are doing something for them in exchange for their fees: *"This week we sent 1,500 copies of your resume to our in-house list of employers."* Many paying clients actually believe they are getting their money's worth. Perhaps in a few days a job will be in the mail for them!

This is the lazy person's way to job search riches.

Many job hunters resort to sending such letters because the broadcast exercise involves motion. It gives them a feeling of doing something about their job search—they are actually contacting potential employers with their resume—without having to go through the process of making personal contacts through referrals and cold calls. Like most direct-mail schemes engaged in by the uninitiated, this is the lazy person's way to job search riches. Just find the names and addresses of several hundred potential employers, address the envelopes and affix postage, and then stuff them with your resume and cover letter. Presto! In a few days you expect phone calls from employers who just discovered your talents by opening their junk mail!

Let's speak the truth about going nowhere with this approach. Motion does mean momentum. Anyone who thinks he or she can get a job by engaging in such a junk mail exercise is at best engaging in a self-fulfilling prophecy: it results in few if any responses and numerous rejections. If you want to experience rejections, or need to fill your weekly depression quota, just broadcast several hundred resumes and letters to employers. Wait a few weeks and you will most likely get the depressing news—no one is positive about you and your resume. At best you will receive a few polite form letters informing you that the employer will keep your resume on file:

> Thank you for sending us your resume. While we do not have a vacancy at present for someone with your qualifications, we will keep your resume on file for future reference.

If after receiving several such replies you conclude it's a tough job market out there, and no one is interested in your qualifications and experience, you're probably correct. Such an approach to communicating your qualifications to employers set you up for failure.

This is not to say that this approach never works. Indeed, some people do get job interviews from such broadcasted cover letters and resumes. The reason they get interviews is not because of the quality of their resume, letter, or mailing list. It's because of dumb luck in playing the numbers game.

Direct-mail operates like this. If you know what you are doing—have an excellent product targeted to a very receptive audience—you may receive a 2% positive response. Indeed, successful direct-mail campaigns use 2% as an indicator of success. On the other hand, if your product is less than exciting and is not well targeted on an audience, you can expect to receive less than .5% positive response. In some cases you may receive no response whatsoever. In fact, few direct-mail campaigns ever result in a 2% response rate!

You should never expect to receive more than a 1% positive response to your broadcast letters and resumes. Translated into real numbers, this means for every 100 unsolicited resumes you mail, you'll be lucky to get one interview. For every 1000 resumes you mail, you may get 10 interviews. But you will be lucky if you even get a 1% positive response. Chances are your efforts will be rewarded with no invitations to interview.

The reason for such meager numbers is simple: you don't have a receptive audience for your mailing piece. Employers are busy and serious people who seek candidates when they have specific personnel needs. If they have no vacancies, why would they be interested in interviewing candidates or even replying to an unsolicited letter and resume for a nonexistent position? Such mail is a waste of their time. Writing responses to such mail costs them time and money. Employers simply don't interview people based upon a survey of their junk mail.

If you do get an interview from a broadcast letter, chances are you got lucky: your letter and resume arrived at the time an employer was actually looking for a candidate with your type of qualifications. This is your luck calling.

If you decide to engage in the broadcast exercise, please don't waste a great deal of time and money trying to produce the "perfect" mailing piece or acquiring a "hot" mailing list. It's wishful thinking that the quality of the mailing piece or your mailing list will somehow give you an "extra edge" in generating a higher response rate.

Employers don't interview people based upon a survey of their junk mail.

Simply write a short three-paragraph cover letter in which you generate interest in both you and your resume as well as demonstrate your enthusiasm, drive, honesty, goals, and performance orientation. The first two paragraphs introduce you to the employer by way of your experience, previous performance, and future goals. The final paragraph calls for action on the part of the receiver:

> I have seven years of progressive sales and marketing experience in pharmaceuticals. Last year alone I generated $3.5 million in annual sales—a 25% increase over the previous year. Next year I want to do at least $4.5 million.

> I'm interested in taking on new challenges with a firm that values team performance and is interested in exploring new markets. As you can see from my enclosed resume, I have extensive sales and marketing experience. For the past five years, I've exceeded my annual sales goals.

> If you have a need for someone with my experience, I would appreciate an opportunity to speak with you about my qualifications and future plans. I can be contacted during the day at 808/729-3290 and in the evening at 808/729-4751.

If this letter were received by an employer who had a specific need for an experienced and productive individual in pharmaceutical sales and marketing, chances are he or she would contact the writer. However, the chances are very slim that this letter would connect with an employer who had such an immediate and specific need. Therefore, this otherwise excellent letter is likely to result in numerous rejections because it has no audience on the day it arrives.

While it is always preferable to address your letter to a specific name and type each envelope rather than use computer-generated mailing labels, in the end it probably doesn't really make much difference if no position exists in reference to your letter and resume. It does make a difference if you are lucky to stumble upon a position through such a mailing effort. An employer either does or does not have a personnel need specifically coinciding with your qualifications and experience. The **content** of both your letter and resume is the most important element in this broadcast exercise. If an employer has a specific personnel need and your letter and resume indicate you fit those needs, you'll probably hear form the employer regardless of whether you have his or her correct name and title or if you used a computer-generated mailing label. The employer knows what you are doing regardless of any cosmetic pretenses to the contrary.

The employer knows what you are doing regardless of any cosmetic pretenses to the contrary.

How effective this mailing piece becomes will depend on your luck. Whatever you do, don't expect to receive many positive responses. And be prepared for an avalanche of bad news—no one appears to want you! You will collect numerous rejections in the process. After you complete this direct mail exercise, get back to what you should really be doing with your job search time—directly contacting potential employers through referral networks, cold calling techniques, and in response to advertised vacancies.

Cover letters targeted to employers with specific personnel needs will result in many more positive responses than the junk mail you generated. You will decrease your number of rejections with a higher number of acceptances.

APPROACH LETTERS

Approach letters are some of the most important letters you should write during your job search. The purpose of these letters is to approach individuals for job search information, advice, and referrals. They play a central role in your prospecting and networking activities. You write them because you need information on alternative jobs, the job market, organizations, potential employers, and job vacancies. You need this information because the job market is highly decentralized and chaotic, and because you want to uncover job leads before others learn about them. Approach letters help you bring some degree of coherence and structure to your job search by organizing the job market around your interests, skills, and experience.

Approach letters are largely responsible for opening doors for informational interviews—one of the most critical interviews in your job search. Approach letters help give you access to important job information and potential employers. Failure to write these letters is likely to weaken your overall job search campaign.

An approach letter should never be accompanied by a resume.

One of the most important differences between approach letters and cover letters is that an approach letter should **never** be accompanied by a resume. The reason is simple: an enclosed resume implies you are looking for a job from the individual who receives your letter. You put responsibility on this individual to either give you a job or help you find one. Few individuals want such responsibility or are eager to become your job search helper. This pushy and presumptuous approach violates the most important principle of the approach letter—these letters are designed for gaining access to critical job search information, advice, and referrals. Such a letter should never imply that you are looking for a job with or through this individual. It's only during an informational interview, preferably **after** you receive such information, advice, and referrals, should you share your resume with your letter recipient.

Time and again job searchers make the mistake of writing an approach letter but enclosing their resume. Such ill-conceived actions generate contradictory messages. While they may produce an outstanding approach letter, they in effect kill it by attaching a resume. The letter says they are only asking for information, advice, and referrals, but the enclosed resume implies they are actually looking for a job from the letter recipient. Such a contradictory message communicates to the recipient that he or she is likely to be abused by what appears to be an unethical or dishonest job seeker. They are unethical or dishonest because they use the approach letter and the informational interview as pretexts for asking for a job. This puts the recipients on the spot and makes them feel uncomfortable.

You may want to write two different types of approach letters for different situations: referral and cold turkey. The **referral approach letter** is written to someone based on a referral or a connection with someone else. A friend or acquaintance, for example, recommends that you contact a particular individual for job search information and advice:

> *"Why don't you contact John Staples. He really knows what's going on. I'm sure he'd be happy to give you advice on what he knows about the pharmaceutical industry in this area. Tell him I recommended that you give him a call."*

This type of referral is **the** basis for building and expanding networks for conducting informational interviews that eventually lead to job interviews and offers. It's the type of referral you want to elicit again and again in the process of expanding your job search network into the offices of potential employers. When you receive such a referral, you have one of two choices for developing the connection.

First, depending on the situation and the individual's position, you may want to immediately initiate the contact by telephone. The use of the telephone is efficient; it gets the job done quickly. However, it is not always the most effective way of initiating a contact. The individual may be very busy and thus unable to take your call, or he may be in the middle of some important business that should not be interrupted by someone like you. When you telephone a stranger, you may face immediate resistance to any attempt to use his valuable time or schedule an informational interview.

Second, you may want to write a referral approach letter. While not as efficient as a telephone call, this letter is likely to be more effective. It prepares the individual for your telephone call. Such a letter enables you to be in complete control of the one-way communication; you should be better able to craft an effective message that will lead to a productive telephone call and informational interview.

This type of approach letter should immediately open with a personal statement that nicely connects you to the reader via your referral and a bit of flattery. Start with something like this:

> John Staples suggested that I contact you regarding the local pharmaceutical industry. He said you know the business better than anyone else.

> When I spoke with Mary Thompson today, she highly recommended you as a source of information on the local pharmaceutical industry.

Such statements include two positives that should result in a favorable impression on the receiver: You've already been screened by the referral for making this contact, and this individual is recognized as an expert in the eyes of others who are important to him who, in turn, pass this recognition on to others.

The next two paragraphs should indicate your interests, motivations, and background in reference to the purpose of making this contact. It should clearly communicate your intentions for making this contact and for using the individual's time. You might say something like this:

> After several successful years in pharmaceutical sales and marketing in Boston, I've decided to relocate to the Midwest where I can be closer to my family. However, having moved to the East nearly 15 years ago, I've discovered I'm somewhat of a stranger to the industry in this area.

> I would very much appreciate any information and advice you might be able to share with me on the nature of the pharmaceutical industry in the greater Chicago Metro area. I have several questions I'm hoping to find answers to in the coming weeks. Perhaps, as John said, you could fill me in on the who, what, and where of the local industry.

Throughout this letter, as well as in your telephone conversation or in a face-to-face meeting, you should **never** indicate that you are looking for a job through this individual. You are only seeking information and advice. If this contact results in referrals that lead to job interviews and offers, that's great. But you are explicitly initiating this contact because you need more information and advice at this stage of your job search. This individual, in effect, becomes your personal advisor—not your future employer. Individuals who use the approach letter for the purpose of getting a job through the recipient abuse this form of communication. Their actions are exploitive, and they tend to become undesirable nuisances few people want to hire. Worst still, they give networking and informational interviewing bad names.

Whatever you do, make sure you are completely honest when you approach referral contacts for information and advice. You will get better cooperation and information as well as be seen as a thoughtful individual who should be promoted through referrals and networking. Therefore, the second and third paragraphs of your letter should indicate your true intentions in initiating this contact.

Your final paragraph should consist of an action statement which indicates what you will do next:

> I've give you a call Tuesday afternoon to see if your schedule would permit some time to discuss my interests in the local pharmaceutical industry. I appreciate your time and look forward to talking with you in a few days.

You—not the letter recipient—must take follow-up action on this letter. You should never end such a letter with an action statement requesting the recipient to contact you (*"I look forward to hearing from you"* or *"Please give me a call if your schedule would permit us to meet"*). If you do, you will not receive a reply. As we will see in Chapter Eight), it's incumbent upon you to further initiate the contact with a telephone call. Assuming you sent the letter by regular first-class mail, try to leave at least four days between when you mailed the letter and when you make the telephone call. If you use special next-day delivery services, make your call on the same delivery day, preferably between 2pm and 4pm.

This action statement prepares the contact for your telephone call and subsequent conversation or meeting. He or she will most likely give you some time. However, please note that this action statement is also a thoughtful conclusion that does not specify the nature of your future contact nor is it overly aggressive or presumptuous (*"I'll schedule a meeting"*). The open-ended statement *"to see if your schedule would permit some time"* could result in either a telephone interview or a face-to-face meeting. In many cases a telephone interview will suffice. The individual may have limited amount of information that is best shared in a 5-10 minute telephone call. In other cases, a face-to-face half-hour to one-hour informational interview would be more appropriate. By choosing such a closing action statement, you leave the time, place, and medium of the interview open to discussion.

The **cold-turkey approach letter** is written for the same purpose but without a personal contact. In this case you literally approach a stranger with no prior contacts. In contrast to the referral approach letter, in this situation you do not have instant credibility attendant with a personal connect. While cold-turkey contacts can be difficult to initiate, they can play an important role in your job search campaign.

Since you do not have a personal contact to introduce you to the letter recipient, you need to begin your letter with an appropriate "cold call" opener that logically connects you to the reader. Try to make your connection as warm, personal, and professional as possible. Avoid excessive flattery or boastful statements that are likely to make your motives suspect and thus turn off the reader. It's always helpful to inject in this letter a personal observation that gently strokes the ego of the reader. If, for example, you read a newspaper article about the individual's work, or if he or she recently received an award or promotion, you might introduce yourself in this letter in any of the following ways:

> I read with great interest about your work with _____.
> Congratulations on a job well done. During the past twelve years I've been involved in similar work.

Congratulations on receiving the annual community development award. Your efforts have certainly help revitalize our downtown area. My interests in urban development began nearly 10 years ago when I was studying urban planning at St. Louis University.

Congratulations on your recent promotion to Vice President of Allied Materials. I've been one of your admirers for the past five years, following your many community and professional activities. Your work in expanding Allied Materials' markets to Japan and China especially interests me because of my previous marketing work in Asia.

Make sure you focus on making a <u>logical connection</u> that is both personal and professional.

Other openers might begin with

I am writing to you because of your position as . . .

Because of your experience in . . .

We have a common interest in . . .

Since we are both alumni of Texas A&M, I thought . . .

As a fellow member of Delta Sigma Alpha sorority, I wanted to congratulate you on your recent election to . . .

Whatever opener you choose, make sure you focus on making a **logical connection** that is both personal and professional. Inject some personality in this letter. After all, you want this stranger to take an immediate interest in you. Try to communicate that you are a likeable, enthusiastic, honest, and competent person worth talking to or even meeting. The very first sentence should grab the reader's attention.

A strong opener in a cold-turkey approach letter can be nearly as effective as the personal contact opener in the referral approach letter.

The remaining paragraphs of the cold-turkey referral letter will be structured similarly to the referral approach letter—indicate your interests, motivations, and background in reference to your purpose in making this contact. Clearly communicate your intentions for making this contact and for using the individual's time. Again, be perfectly honest and tactful in what you say, but avoid making honest but stupid statements, such as *"I really don't know what's going to happen to me in the next three months."* Be sure to close with an indication of action—you will call on a particular date to see if the person's schedule would permit some time to discuss your interests.

If you incorporate these two types of approach letters in your job search, you will quickly discover they are the most powerful forms of communication in your job search arsenal. They must be written and targeted toward individuals who have information, advice, and referrals relevant to your job search interests. They are the bricks and mortar for building networks that generate informational interviews that lead to job interviews and offers. Resumes and telephone calls are no substitute for these referral letters. A resume **never** accompanies these letters, and a telephone call only follows **after** the recipient has received and read your approach letter. If you write these letters according to our suggested structure and content and follow-up with the telephone call, you will receive a great deal of useful job search information, advice, and referrals. You will learn about the structure of the job market, identify key players who can help you, and inject a healthy dose of reality into a job search that may otherwise be guided by myths and wishful thinking.

If for any reason you still feel compelled to sneak a resume in the envelope with one of these approach letters, you will quickly discover few recipients want to see or talk with you. The enclosed resume immediately transforms what was potentially an effective approach letter into an ineffective cover letter for a job application—something that is inappropriate in this situation. As we've already seen, an effective cover letter has a different purpose as well as follows other writing, distribution, and follow-up principles.

THANK-YOU LETTERS

Thank-you letters are some of the most effective communications in a job search. They demonstrate an important **social grace** that says something about you as an individual—your personality and how you probably relate to others. They communicate one of the most important characteristics sought in potential employees—**thoughtfulness**.

Better still, since few individuals write thank-you letters, those who do write them are **remembered** by letter recipients. And one thing you definitely want to happen again and again during your job search is to be remembered by individuals who can provide you with useful information, advice, and referrals as well as invite you to job interviews and extend to you job offers. Being remembered as a thoughtful person with the proper social graces will give you an edge over many other job seekers who fail to write thank-you letters. Whatever you do, make sure you regularly send thank-you letters in response to individuals who assist you in your job search.

Being remembered as a thoughtful person with the proper social graces will give you an edge over many other job seekers.

Many job seekers discover the most important letters they ever wrote were thank-you letters. These letters can have several positive outcomes:

- **Contacts turn into more contacts and job interviews:** A job seeker sends a thank-you letter to someone who recommended they contact a former college roommate; impressed with the thoughtfulness of the job seeker and feeling somewhat responsible for helping her make the right contacts, the individual continues providing additional referrals, which eventually lead to two job interviews.

- **Job interview turns into a job offer:** A job seeker completes a job interview. Within 24-hours he writes a nice thank-you in which he expresses his gratitude for having an opportunity to interview for the position as well as reiterates his interest in working for the employer. This individual is subsequently offered the job. The employer later tells him it was his thoughtful thank-you letter that gave him the edge over two other equally qualified candidates who never bothered to follow-up the interview.

- **A job rejection later turns into a job offer:** After interviewing for a position, a job seeker receives a standard rejection letter from an employer indicating the job was offered to another individual. Rather than get angry and end communications with the employer, the job seeker sends a nice thank-you letter in which she notes her disappointment in not being selected and then thanks him for the opportunity to interview for the position. She also reiterates her continuing interest in working for the organization. The employer remembers this individual. Rather than let her get away, he decides to create a new position for her.

- **A job offer turns into an immediate positive relationship:** Upon receiving a job offer, the new employee sends a nice thank-you letter in which he expresses his appreciation for the confidence expressed by the employer. He also reassures the employer that he will be as productive as expected. This letter is well received by the employer who is looking forward to working closely with such a thoughtful new employee. Indeed, he becomes a mentor and sponsor who immediately gives the employee some plum assignments that help him fast-track his career within the organization.

- **Termination results in strong recommendations and a future job offer:** An employee, seeking to advance her career with a larger organization, receives a job offer from a completing firm. In submitting her formal letter of resignation, she also sends a personal thank-you letter to her former employer. She sincerely expresses her gratitude for having the opportunity work with him and attributes much of her success to his mentoring. This letter further confirms his conclusion about this former employee—he's loosing a valuable asset. While he can not offer her a similar or better career opportunity in this organization, he will keep her in mind if things change. And things do change two years later when he makes a major career move to a much larger organization. One of the first things he does as Vice-President is to begin shaping his own personal staff. He immediately contacts her to see if she would be interested in working with him. She's interested and soon joins her former employer in making another major career move.

In these cases it was the job seekers' thank-you letters, rather than their cover letters and resumes, that got them job interviews and offers.

As indicated in the above scenarios, thank-you letters should be written in the following situations:

- **After receiving information, advice, or a referral from a contact:** You should always express your gratitude in writing to individuals who provide you with job search assistance. Not only is this a nice thing to do, it also is functional for a successful job search. Individuals who feel they are appreciated will most likely remember you and be willing to further assist you with your job search and recommend you to others.

- **Immediately after interviewing for a job:** Whether it be a telephone or face-to-face interview, always write a nice thank-you letter within 12-hours of completing the interview. This letter should express your gratitude for having an opportunity to interview for the job. Be sure to reiterate your interest in the job and stress your possible contributions to the employer's operations. The letter should emphasize your major strengths in relationship to the employer's needs. All other things being equal, this letter may give you an "extra edge" over other candidates. It may well prove to be your most effective letter in your entire job search!

- **Withdrawing from further consideration:** At some point during the recruitment process, you may decide to withdraw from further consideration. Perhaps you decided to take another job, you're now more satisfied with your present job, or the position no longer interests you. For whatever reason, you should write a short thank-you letter in which you withdraw from consideration. Explain in positive terms why you are no longer interested in pursuing an application with the organization. Thank them for their time and consideration.

- **After receiving a rejection:** Even if you receive a rejection, it's a good idea to write a thank-you letter. How many employers ever receive such a letter from what ostensibly should be a disappointed job seeker? This unique letter is likely to be remembered—which is what you want to accomplish in this situation. Being remembered may result in referrals to other employers or perhaps a job interview and offer at some later date.

- **After receiving a job offer:** However well they think they hire, employers still are uncertain about the outcome of their hiring decisions until new employees perform in their organization. Why not put their initial anxieties to ease and get off on the right foot by writing a nice thank-you letter? In this letter express your appreciation for having received the confidence and trust of the employer. Reiterate what you told the employer during the job interview(s) about your goals and expected performance. Conclude with a reaffirmation of your starting date as well as a statement about how much you look forward to becoming a productive member of the team. Such a thoughtful letter will be well received by the employer. It could well accelerate your progress within the organization beyond the norm.

■ **Upon leaving a job:** Whether you leave your job voluntarily or are forced by circumstances to terminate, try to leave a positive part of you behind by writing a thank-you letter. Burning bridges behind you through face-to-face confrontation or a vindictive, get-even letter may later catch up with you, especially if you anger someone in the process who may later be in a position to affect your career. If you quit to take a job with another organization, thank your employer for the time you spent with the organization and the opportunities given to you to acquire valuable experience and skills. If you terminated under difficult circumstances—organizational cutbacks or a nasty firing—try to leave on as positive a note as possible. Employers in such situations would rather have you out of sight and mind. Assure them there are no hard feelings, and you wish them the best as you would hope they would wish you the same. Stress the positives of your relationship with both the employer and the organization. Remember, your future employer may call your previous employer for information on your past performance. If you leave a stressful situation on a positive note, chances are your previous employer will give you the benefit of the doubt and stress only your positives to others. He may even commit a few "sins of omission" that only you and he know about: *"She ready worked well with her co-workers and was one of our best analysts"* does not tell the whole story which may be that you couldn't get along with your boss, and vice versa. After having made peace with each other through the medium of the thank-you letter, what would your former employer have to gain by telling the whole story to others about your work with him? Your thank-you letter should at least neutralize the situation and at best turn a negative situation into a positive for your career. Indeed, he may well become one of your supporters—for other jobs with other employers, that is!

Examples of each type of letter, written according to our principles of effective thank-you letters, appear at the end of this chapter and are identified accordingly.

Thank-you letters should always be written in a timely manner. Make it a practice to sit down and write these letters within 12-hours of the situation that prompts this letter. It should be mailed immediately so that it reaches the recipient within three to four days. If you wait longer, the letter will have less impact on the situation. Indeed, in the case of the interview thank-you letter, if an employer is making a final hiring decision among three candidates, your letter should arrive as soon as possible to affect the outcome.

Whether you handwrite or type this letter may not make a great deal of difference in terms of outcomes, but your choice says something about your professional style and mentality. Many people claim handwritten thank-you letters are more powerful than typed letters. We doubt such claims and have yet to see any credible data on the subject other than personal preferences and questionable logic. It is true that handwritten thank-you letters communicate a certain personal element that cannot be expressed in typewritten letters. If you choose to handwrite this letter, make sure you have attractive handwriting. Your handwriting form and style could be a negative.

The problem with handwritten letters is that they can express a certain nonprofessional, amateurish style. They also may raise questions about your motivations and manipulative style. They turn off some readers who expect a business letter, rather than an expression of social graces, in reference to a business situation. Furthermore, some readers may consider the handwritten letter an attempt at psychological manipulation—they know what you're trying to do by handwriting a letter. That's what real estate and car salespeople are taught to do in their training seminars! When in doubt, it's best to type this letter in a neat, clean, and professional manner. If typewritten, such a personal letter also will express your professional style and respond to the expectations appropriate for the situation. It tells the reader that you know proper business etiquette, you know this is a business situation, you are equipped to respond, and you attempt to demonstrate your best professional effort.

RESUME LETTERS

A resume letter is a special type of approach letter that substitutes for a formal resume. Merging the cover letter and resume into a single document, this type of letter is written when it is appropriate to target your qualifications in a format other than a separate cover letter and resume. It's most often used to approach employers with information on your experience and skills in the hope that they will have vacancies for someone with your qualifications.

Since it outlines your experience and skills, the resume letter is designed to get job interviews with employers. It, in effect, asks for a job interview rather than information, advice, or referrals for expanding your job search.

Similar to the cold-turkey approach letter, the resume letter should open with a logical connection between you and the employer. The second paragraph, however, is what defines this as a resume letter. This paragraph should summarize your major experience and skills in relation to the employer's needs. In fact, you may want to take this section directly from the "Areas of Effectiveness," "Experience," or "Work History" section appearing on your resume. For ease of reading, it's best to bullet each item, preferably including three to five items similar to the examples found at the end of this chapter. The final paragraph should call for action—you taking the initiative to call the recipient at a specific time for the purpose of scheduling a possible interview.

You should try to keep this letter to a single page. Remember, it is neither a cover letter nor a resume, but a combination of both which has a specific purpose—you are trying to invite yourself to a job interview. Since this type of letter tends to put employers on the spot—here's another cold-call job applicant—it will probably generate few positive responses and numerous rejections. However well written this letter may be, few employers are prepared to give job interviews based on such a letter. Chances are most employers will not have vacancies available at the time you send this letter. What they may be able to do is give you referrals to other employers who may have vacancies—but only if you follow-up this letter with a phone call. In the end, your resume letter may become an important prospecting letter for uncovering job leads.

COVER LETTER
Response to Advertised Position

2842 South Plaza
Chicago, IL 60228

March 12, _____

David C. Johnson
Director of Personnel
Bank of Chicago
490 Michigan Avenue
Chicago, IL 60222

Dear Mr. Johnson:

The accompanying resume is in response to your listing in yesterday's Chicago Tribune for a loan officer.

I am especially interested in this position because my experience with the Small Business Administration has prepared me for understanding the financial needs and problems of the business community from the perspectives of both lenders and borrowers. I wish to use this experience with a growing and community-conscious bank such as yours.

I would appreciate an opportunity to meet with you to discuss how my experience will best meet your needs. My ideas on how to improve small business financing may be of particular interest to you. I will call your office on the morning of March 17 to inquire if a meeting can be scheduled at a convenient time.

I look forward to meeting you.

Sincerely yours,

Joyce Pitman

COVER LETTER
Referral

2237 South Olby Road
Sacramento, CA 97342

July 17, ____

David Myers
Vice President
Fulton Engineering Corporation
1254 Madison Street
Sacramento, CA 97340

Dear Mr. Myers:

John Bird, the Director of Data Systems at Ottings Engineering Company, informed me that you are looking for someone to direct your new management information system.

I enclose my resume for your consideration. During the past 10 years I have developed and supervised a variety of systems. I have worked at both the operational and managerial levels and know how to develop systems appropriate for different types of organizations.

I would appreciate an opportunity to visit with you and examine your operations. Perhaps I could provide you with a needs assessment prior to an interview. I will call you next week to make arrangements for a visit.

Thank you for your consideration.

Sincerely,

Gary S. Platt

APPROACH LETTER
Referral

1099 Seventh Avenue
Akron, OH 44522

December 10, _____

Janet L. Cooper, Director
Architectural Design Office
RT Engineering Associates
621 West Grand Avenue
Akron, OH 44520

Dear Ms. Cooper:

John Sayres suggested that I write to you in regards to my interests in architectural drafting. He thought you would be a good person to give me some career advice.

I am interested in an architectural drafting position with a firm specializing in commercial construction. As a trained draftsman, I have six years of progressive experience in all facets of construction, from pouring concrete to developing plans for $14 million in commercial and residential construction. I am particularly interested in improving construction design and building operations of shopping complexes.

Mr. Sayres mentioned you as one of the leading experts in this growing field. Would it be possible for us to meet briefly? Over the next few months I will be conducting a job search. I am certain your counsel would assist me as I begin looking for new opportunities.

I will call your office next week to see if your schedule permits such a meeting.

Sincerely,

John Albert

APPROACH LETTER
Cold Turkey

2189 West Church Street
New York, NY 10011

May 3, _____

Patricia Dotson, Director
Northeast Association for
  the Elderly
9930 Jefferson Street
New York, NY 10013

Dear Ms. Dotson:

I have been impressed with your work with the elderly. Your organization takes a community perspective in trying to integrate the concerns of the elderly with those of other community groups. Perhaps other organizations will soon follow your lead.

I am anxious to meet you and learn more about your work. My background with the city Volunteer Services Program involved frequent contact with elderly volunteers. From this experience I decided I preferred working primarily with the elderly.

However, before I pursue my interest further, I need to talk to people with experience in gerontology. In particular, I would like to know more about careers with the elderly as well as how my background might best be used in the field of gerontology.

In am hoping you can assist me in this matter. I would like to meet with you briefly to discuss several of my concerns. I will call next week to see if your schedule permits such a meeting.

I look forward to meeting you.

Sincerely,

Carol Timms

THANK-YOU LETTER
Referral

9821 West Fulton Street
Miami, FL 30303

March 7, _____

Martin Davis
213 Doreen Drive
Miami, FL 30301

Dear Martin,

Thanks so much for putting me in contact with Jane Burton at Fordham Manufacturing Company.

I spoke with her today about my interests in technical training. She was most gracious with her time and provided me with a great deal of useful information on job opportunities in the Miami area. She even made some valuable suggestions for strengthening my resume and gave me a few names of individuals who might be interested in my qualifications.

I'll send you a copy of my resume once I revise it. Please feel free to make any comments or suggestions as well as share it with others who might be interested in my background.

Again, thanks so much for putting me in contact with Jane Burton. She spoke very highly of you and your work with the United Fund.

Sincerely,

Steven Zolbert

THANK-YOU LETTER
After Informational Interview

9910 Thompson Drive
Cleveland, OH 43382

June 21, _____

Jane Evans, Director
Evans Finance Corporation
2122 Forman Street
Cleveland, OH 43380

Dear Ms. Evans:

Your advice was most helpful in clarifying my questions on careers in finance. I am now reworking my resume and have included many of your thoughtful suggestions. I will send you a copy next week.

Thanks so much for taking time from your busy schedule to see me. I will keep in contact and follow through on your suggestion to see Sarah Cook about opportunities with the Cleveland-Akron Finance Company.

Sincerely,

Daryl Haines

THANK-YOU LETTER
Post Job Interview

2962 Forrest Drive
Denver, CO 82171

May 28, _____

Thomas F. Harris
Director, Personnel Department
Coastal Products Incorporated
7229 Lakewood Drive
Denver, CO 82170

Dear Mr. Harris:

Thank you again for the opportunity to interview for the marketing position. I appreciated your hospitality and enjoyed meeting you and members of your staff.

The interview convinced me of how compatible my background, interests, and skills are with the goals of Coastal Products Incorporated. My prior marketing experience with the Department of Commerce has prepared me to take a major role in developing both domestic and international marketing strategies. I am confident my work could result in increased market shares for Coastal Products Incorporated in the rapidly expanding Pacific Rim market.

For more information on the new product promotion program I mentioned, call David Garrett at the Department of Commerce; his number is 202/726-0132. I talked to Dave this morning and mentioned your interest in this program.

I look forward to meeting you and your staff again.

Sincerely,

Stephanie Potter

THANK-YOU LETTER
Responding to Rejection

1947 Grace Avenue
Springfield, MA 01281

September 14, _____

Sharon T. Avery
Vice President for Sales
Bentley Enterprises
529 W. Sheridan Road
Washington, DC 20011

Dear Ms. Avery:

Thank you for giving me the opportunity to interview for the Customer Services Representative position. I appreciate your consideration and interest in me. I learned a great deal from our meetings.

Although I am disappointed in not being selected for your current vacancy, I want you to know that I appreciated the courtesy and professionalism shown to me during the entire selection process. I enjoyed meeting you, John Roberts, and other members of your sales staff. My meetings confirmed that Bentley Enterprises would be an exciting place to work and build a career.

I want to reiterate my strong interest in working for you. Please keep me in mind should another position become available in the near future.

Again, thank you for the opportunity to interview. Best wishes to you and your staff.

Yours truly,

Gail S. Topper

THANK-YOU LETTER
Withdrawing From Consideration

733 Main Street
Williamsburg, VA 23512

December 1, _____

Dr. Thomas C. Bostelli, President
Northern States University
2500 University Drive
Greenfield, MA 03241

Dear Dr. Bostelli:

It was indeed a pleasure meeting with you and your staff last week to discuss your need for a Director of Public and Government Relations. Our time together was most enjoyable and informative.

As I discussed with you during our meetings, I believe one purpose of preliminary interviews is to explore areas of mutual interest and to assess the fit between the individual and the position. After careful consideration, I have decided to withdraw from consideration for the position.

My decision is based upon several factors. First, the emphasis on fund raising is certainly needed, but I would prefer more balance in my work activities. Second, the position would require more travel than I am willing to accept with my other responsibilities. Third, professional opportunities for my husband would be very limited in northwest Massachusetts.

I want to thank you for interviewing me and giving me the opportunity to learn about your needs. You have a fine staff and faculty, and I would have enjoyed working with them.

Best wishes in your search.

Sincerely,

Janet L. Lawson

THANK-YOU LETTER
Accepting Job Offer

7694 James Courts
San Francisco, CA 94826

June 7, _____

Judith Greene
Vice President
West Coast Airlines
2400 Van Ness
San Francisco, CA 94829

Dear Ms. Greene:

I am pleased to accept your offer, and I am looking forward to joining you and your staff next month.

The customer relations position is ideally suited to my background and interests. I assure you I will give you my best effort in making this an effective position within your company.

I understand I will begin work on July 1. If, in the meantime, I need to complete any paper work or take care of any other matters, please contact me at 377-4029.

I enjoyed meeting with you and your staff and appreciated the professional manner in which the hiring was conducted.

Sincerely,

Joan Kitner

THANK-YOU LETTER
Terminating Employment

1099 Seventh Avenue
Akron, OH 44522

August 2, _____

Mr. James T. Thomas
Chief Engineer
Akron Construction Company
1170 South Hills Highway
Akron, OH 44524

Dear Jim,

I am writing to inform you that I will be leaving Akron Construction Company on September 12 to accept another position.

As you know, I have developed an interest in architectural drafting which combines my drafting skills with my artistic interests. While I was vacationing in Houston recently, a relative approached me about an opening for someone with my background with a large architecture and engineering firm. I investigated the possibility and, consequently, received an offer. After careful consideration, I decided to accept the offer and relocate to Houston. I will be working with Brown and Little Company.

I have thoroughly enjoyed working with you over the past two years, and deeply appreciate your fine supervision and support. You have taught me a great deal about drafting, and I want to thank you for providing me with the opportunity to work here. It has been a very positive experience for me both personally and professionally.

I wanted to give you more than the customary two weeks notice so you would have time to find my replacement. I made the decision to relocate yesterday and decided to inform you immediately.

Best wishes.

Sincerely,

John Albert

RESUME LETTER

773 Main Street
Williamsburg, VA 23572

November 12, _____

Barbara Thompson, President
SRM Associates
421 91st Street
New York, NY 11910

Dear Ms. Thompson:

I just completed reading the article in Business Today on SRM Associates. Your innovative approach to recruiting minorities is of particular interest to me because of my background in public relations and minority recruitment.

I am interested in learning more about your work as well as the possibilities of joining your firm. My qualifications include:

- research and writing on minority recruitment and medical education
- secured funding and administered $845,000 minority representation program
- published several professional articles and reports on creative writing, education, and minorities
- organized and led public relations, press, and minority conferences
- M.A. in Journalism and B.A. in English

I will be in New York City during the week of December 10. Perhaps your schedule would permit us to meet briefly to discuss our mutual interests. I will call your office next week to see if such a meeting can be arranged.

I appreciate your consideration.

Sincerely yours,

Michael R. Folger

RESUME LETTER

4921 Tyler Drive
Washington, DC 20011

March 15, ____

Doris Stevens
STR Corporation
179 South Trail
Rockville, MD 21101

Dear Ms. Stevens:

STR Corporation is one of the most dynamic computer companies in the nation. Its model employee training and development program makes it the type of organization I am interested in joining.

I am seeking a training position with a computer firm which would use my administrative, communication, and planning abilities to develop effective training and counseling programs. My experience includes:

Administration: Supervised instructors and counselors. Coordinated job vacancy and training information for businesses and schools.

Communication: Conducted over 100 workshops on interpersonal skills, stress management, and career planning. Frequent guest speaker to various agencies and private firms. Experienced writer of training manuals and public relations materials.

Planning: Planned and developed counseling programs for over 5,000 employees. Reorganized interviewing and screening processes and developed program of individualized and group counseling.

I am also completing my Ph.D. in industrial psychology with an emphasis on developing training and counseling programs for technical personnel.

Could we meet to discuss your program as well as how my experience might relate to your needs? I will call your office on Tuesday morning, March 23, to arrange a convenient time.

I especially want to show you a model employee counseling and career development program I recently developed. Perhaps you may find it useful for your work with STR.

Sincerely,

James C. Astor

Chapter Four

FORM, STRUCTURE, AND DESIGN

Effective letter writing is hard yet rewarding work. It involves much more than just sticking a piece of paper in the typewriter or turning on a wordprocessor, pounding out a few sentences and paragraphs, and depositing the product in a mail box. Above all, it requires knowledge about the elements of effective communication and the reading behavior of busy letter recipients.

EFFECTIVE COMMUNICATION

Most individuals receiving your letters are busy people. Indeed, many hiring officials are inundated with letters and resumes. Some receive over 500 letters a week, but they only have an hour or less a day, interspersed with numerous telephone calls and meetings, to read all their mail.

What would you do if you were faced with such volume of written communication? Busy people simply don't have the time nor motivation to read every word on the page and then sit back and contemplate what they should do next in response to each letter. No wonder many letter writers never receive responses to their job search letters!

Most high-volume letter recipients find shortcuts that help them dispose of each letter within a few seconds (5-10 seconds) so they will have time (30-60 seconds) to read only the most interesting ones. Such seemingly superficial elements as the general "look" of the envelope and letter—its form, structure, layout—color and weight of paper, type style, salutation, and signature are the first things readers see. How these elements come together to communicate a professional image is important in determining whether or not your reader decides to discard your letter or continue reading for its content.

The old adage that *"you never have a second chance to make a good first impression"* applies equally to job search letters as it does to individuals invited to job interviews. Whatever you do, make sure all elements in your letter make a good first impression so your letter will receive the attention its contents require.

Whatever you do, make sure all elements in your letter make a good first impression so your letter will receive the attention its contents require.

If you want your letters to be most effective—read and responded to—you need to make several important decisions concerning form, content, and distribution. Going beyond standard formats and models of so-called "good letters," you must be creative and thoughtful in planning and organizing your message. You must develop an appropriate form and style, structure appealing content, make important production and distribution decisions, and follow-up on the results of your communication. These are important and time consuming decisions. Failure to deal with any one of them will most likely result in ineffective job search communication. You will have difficulty communicating your qualifications to employers.

Like other types of letters, job search letters should follow certain principles of effective form, structure, and design. While they say nothing about content or the details of your message, these letter writing elements nonetheless help communicate your message to the reader. Without strong form, structure, and design, your letters may become uninviting to the reader. Consider, for example, the hiring official who must review hundreds of letters and resumes each week. The most appealing letters exhibit strong elements of form, structure, and design. Essentially cosmetic in nature, these elements are the first ones communicated to the reader. They determine whether or not the reader will read the letter. If you neglect these elements, your letters may never pass the initial five second test of busy people—does it look interesting enough to invest the next minute of my time reading it?

FORM AND STRUCTURE

What form should you use? Is there one best way to structure the letter? What about my writing style? These questions frequently arise during the initial stages of learning how to write effective correspondence. And the answers to these questions continue to change depending on the goal of your writing and intended audience.

These is no one best form or style to use in letter writing. Instead, there are many alternatives to choose from, plus a great deal of flexibility permitted in being different, unique, and unusual. The business world tends to encourage flexibility and experimentation in most forms of communication. However, this should not be taken as a license to do anything you want to do. You must know your purpose, your audience, and your alternative forms and styles before choosing one that is most appropriate for your particular situation.

Let's examine some standard alternative formats. Most letters include the following elements in their layout:

1. Heading
2. Date line
3. Inside address
4. Salutation or greeting
5. Body of letter

6. Closing
7. Signature lines
8. Identification initials
9. Enclosures
10. Copy reference
11. Postscript (P.S.)

The first seven elements are required for all business letters. The last four elements are optional depending on your particular situation; they seldom appear on job search letters. Each element should be laid out in the sequence as outlined on page 76. The particular style of the layout can vary. We'll discuss style variations when we examine typing styles.

The structure of each letter element follows strict rules, although some variation is permitted in a few cases. When in doubt about a particular rule or its variation, make a decision based upon your understanding of the purpose of the letter—communicate your best professional image with impact. Your common sense may dictate the best course to take.

When writing job search letters, it is inappropriate to use your present employer's letterhead.

---

1. Heading

Letters have two types of headings. The first is **letterhead** or a heading preprinted on company stationery or with an individual's name and address. When writing job search letters, it is inappropriate to use your present employer's letterhead. Doing so communicates the wrong message to a potential future employer—you abuse employers' resources. In addition, potential employers may call you at work, which could prove embarrassing if you are trying to keep your job search secret. Personal letterhead

STANDARD LETTER ELEMENTS

1. heading
2. date line
3. inside address
4. salutation
5. body
6. closing
7. signature line
8. identification initials
9. enclosures
10. copy reference
11. postscript

stationery can look very professional, especially if it is printed with raised letters on 20 lb. bond white, off white, or light grey paper. However, it is not necessary to go to the expense of personalized stationery. It may look a bit extravagant to some employers.

The second type of heading is the **standard plain letter form**. Since nothing is preprinted on the stationery, the writer supplies his or her contact information beginning near the top-right-center of the stationery. The contact information includes only the address immediately followed by a date line:

> 973 W. 191st Street
> Kent, WA 93201
>
> January 27, 1992

2. Date Line

The date line comes immediately after the heading. It should appear in one of two forms: month-day-year or day-month-year:

September 11, 1992

11 September 1992

The month-day-year form is used most commonly in the United Sates. The day-month-year is the standard form used in international communications.

Always write the date in full. Do not abbreviate. It's best to leave one space between the heading and the date line as outlined in our example above and on the previous page.

3. Inside Address

The inside address consists of the title, name, position, company, and address of the organization receiving your letter. The following rules should be followed:

TITLE:	Always address your letter recipient by his or her proper gender or professional title. You have several alternatives depending on whom you are writing to:

Mr.	male
Mrs.	married female
Miss	unmarried female
Ms.	female if unsure of marital status
Messrs.*	more than one male
Mesdames*	more than one married female
Misses*	more than one unmarried female
Dr.	a Doctor of Medicine (M.D.) or Doctor of Philosophy (Ph.D.)

* Correct form, but seldom used.

NAME:	Always try to address your letter to a specific person by name. Write the name in full—no nicknames, shortened forms, or abbreviations other than the middle initial or preferred usage by the individuals. "Dick" should be "Richard"; "Bob" should be "Robert"; "Jim" and "Jimmy" should be "James."
POSITION:	This is normally one's job title within the organization, such as Chairman, President, Chief of Personnel, Division Head.
COMPANY:	Complete name of the organization, including any subdivision such as departments, sections, and offices.
ADDRESS:	Street, post office box, city, state, zip code.

The principles of a proper inside address are illustrated in this example:

Mr. James L. Tone
Chairman of the Board
Renkel Industries, Inc.
462 Fairfax Street
San Francisco, CA 92101

4. Salutation

The salutation or greeting should consist of the greeting "Dear" followed by the proper gender or professional title and surname of the individual. Unless you are a close friend, never address the individual by a first name. Such a familial greeting is inappropriate for job search letters. A colon—not a comma—always follows the individual's last name:

Dear Ms. Stevens:

In most cases you will have a name to address your letter to or you can easily find the name by calling an organization and asking *"To whom should I send my letter?"* However, sometimes you will respond to a classified ad or job vacancy announcement which does not provide a name. The same is true if you broadcast letters to hundreds of anonymous employers. In these cases you should select one of the following alternatives:

- **Omit the salutation altogether.** This is our preference since the employer didn't bother to identify to whom the letter should be addressed. Don't worry, your letter will be delivered to the right person since you already have a title or department identified in your inside address. Omitting the salutation avoids the problem of addressing a gender-sensitive person with the wrong title.

- **Try to neutralize a gender title by using**

  Dear Sir or Madam:
  Dear Sir/Madam:

  However awkward, these are generally acceptable ways of addressing anonymous readers. Avoid addressing your reader as "Dear Gentleperson", "Dear Gentlepeople", "Dear Person", "Dear

Sir", "Dear Ladies and Gentlemen", "Dear Future Employer", "Dear Friend", "Dear Company", "Dear Personnel Department", or "To Whom It May Concern". While they may appear more "correct" than the above titles, they're silly, insensitive, or presumptuous. If you can't do better than our examples, proceed to the body of the letter minus the salutation.

■ **Use an attention line or a subject line.** Attention lines are used for quickly routing a letter to the proper reader. Subject lines are used for quick reference, routing, and filing purposes. You can use either in combination with a salutation—both before and after—or as a substitute for a salutation. In combination, these lines would appear as follows:

> Department of Personnel
> XYZ Corporation
> 1234 Mount Pleasant
> Chicago, IL 60000
>
> ATTENTION: Director of Personnel
>
> Dear Director:
>
> SUBJECT: Area manager position

You can also use them alone or as a substitute for the traditional salutation. Instead of beginning with "Dear Sir/Madam", for example, start with "ATTENTION: Director of Personnel" or "SUBJECT: Area manager position". Attention and subject lines are especially helpful in routing letters within large organizations that recruit for numerous positions.

5. Body and Continuation Pages

The body of your letter normally should be organized so it fits on a single page. The following structural rules should be observed with writing this section:

- **Subdivide the letter into two to four paragraphs:** A single paragraph says too little and more than four paragraphs begins to include too many ideas. Keep the letter simple and to the point by only addressing three or four points.

- **Avoid lengthy paragraphs of more than five lines:** Long paragraphs look uninviting, are hard to follow, and are often cluttered with too many ideas. Five line paragraphs that include two to three sentences per paragraph will serve you well.

- **Keep most sentences to 25 words or less.** Similar to long paragraphs, long sentences are uninviting and are often hard to follow. Keep your sentences simple and to the point.

If you must go beyond one page, your continuation pages should be referenced in some manner. Make sure your continuation pages are always connected with the first page so it cannot be confused with other letters. The most formal and complete continuation page form is to include the addressee's name, the page number, and date near the top of the continuation pages. For example,

```
Carol Johnson                    -2-              April 5, 1992
```

Other forms are also acceptable as long as they look attractive and professional, and include sufficient information for easy reference. For example,

```
Carol Johnson                                         -2-
April 4, 1992
```

Johnson: April 4, 1992   -2-

Leave one inch of blank space above and four single-spaced lines below, this reference information:

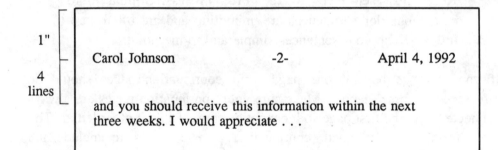

1"

4
lines

Carol Johnson   -2-   April 4, 1992

and you should receive this information within the next three weeks. I would appreciate . . .

6. Closing

Your complimentary close can take various forms. The most standard and formal ones are

Sincerely,
Sincerely yours,
Yours truly,
Very truly yours,
Cordially,
Cordially yours,
Faithfully,
Faithfully yours,
Respectfully,
Respectfully yours,

On the other hand, it is acceptable to be a little more creative with your closings. If, for example, the purpose of your letter is to request information or action from the addressee, you might use one of these closings which re-emphasize the purpose of your letter:

> Hopefully,
> Waiting anxiously your reply,
> Thanking you in advance,
> Appreciatively,
> Gratefully,
> Requesting your assistance,

If you are withdrawing from consideration or turning down a job offer, you might end with some other type of creative closing:

> Regretfully,
> Apologetically,
> Wishing my situation were different,
> So sorry to pass on this,
> Perhaps some other time,

Indeed, such nontraditional, creative closings may be more effective than the traditional formal closings. They make you and your letter stand out as different from the more routine and conformist business letter.

7. Signature Line

Your signature information should be on two lines. Your printed name should appear four spaces below the closing and your actual signature between the closing and printed name. If you don't reference your telephone number in the body of the letter, put it immediately after your name:

> Sincerely,
>
>
> Susan Thomas
> Tel. 801/723-9851

Normally you should not over-formalize your signature information by assigning such titles to you as Mr., Mrs., Miss, and Ms. These titles tend to communicate greater social distance than you want to indicate to others. If, however, you have a professional title, such as "Dr.", you may want to include it with your signature information in order to emphasize your educational and professional background. In this case "Dr." should be specified with the proper initials after your name as either "Ph.D." or "M.D."

Susan Thomas, M.D.

Susan Thomas, Ph.D.

If you want to make your letter more personal, sign only your first name but type your full name. Use this personal approach only after you have established a relationship with someone by phone, letter, or in person—but not in your first encounter.

It's always more impressive to sign your name the old fashioned way— with a fountain pen rather than a ball point pen.

It's always more impressive to sign your name the old fashioned way— with a fountain pen rather than a ball point pen. Blue fountain pen ink contrasts nicely with black type and most paper colors. Fountain pen ink is still the sign of a professional and it adds a touch of class to the whole letter writing process. Be sure your signature looks strong and confident.

8. Identification Initials

This is the first of four optional elements appearing in business letters. While these elements each serve an important function, their absence would not significantly alter the form, substance, or impact of your letters.

Identification initials are included when someone other than the sender transcribed/types the letter. The initials document who did the final production of the letter. These initials take on various acceptable forms with the writer's initials always first, immediately followed by the initials of the transcriber/typist:

> TRS:AF   or   TRS/AF
>
> trs:af   or   trs/af
>
> TRSmith/af
>
> Terrence R. Smith
> AF

Normally, however, one does not have a secretary type a job search letter.

9. Enclosures

If you include some item or items with your letter, such as your resume, make an "Enclosure" reference immediately after the identification initials. If more than one item is enclosed, specify the number after the word "Enclosure." This reference again documents who did what, and is important should the enclosures be missing, which sometimes happens. Proper forms include

> TRS:AF
> Enclosure
>
> TRS:AF
> Enclosures 2

10. Copy Reference

If a copy of your letter is also being sent to another party or parties, use a copy reference to indicate who is receiving the additional copies. The proper forms to use are these:

TRS:AF
cc: James Olson

TRS:AF
Enclosures 3
cc: James Olson
    Mary Davis

11. Using Postscripts (P.S.)

Postscripts are used to include additional information in your letter. While it is acceptable to include postscripts, we only recommend using them under special circumstances. Postscripts tend to imply disorganized afterthoughts which distract the reader from your main message; they often convey lack of professionalism. Some writers use them improperly as dumping grounds for disconnected thoughts. On the other hand, some postscripts are useful to include, especially if your purpose is to re-emphasize or highlight an important point. This most often occurs in the case of sales letters where the writer's purpose is to make a final appeal or present a special last minute offer. In such a situation a postscript gives the letter added impact.

*Postscripts should only be used if
they strengthen the impact
of your message.*

The postscript should begin two spaces following the identification initials, enclosure, or copy reference—whichever comes last. It might be written as follows:

P.S. John Davis asked me to send his regards.

P.S. I will be in your area Tuesday afternoon.

P.S. I will be out of town February 7-10.

Remember to use postscripts sparingly. Postscripts should only be used if they strengthen the impact of your message. If you forget to include certain information in the body of your letter, by all means retype the letter with the information included in the body rather than put it in a postscript as a disorganized after-thought.

TYPING STYLES

Several typing styles are acceptable for business letters. You have four major choices:

- Fully-blocked style
- Square-blocked style
- Modified-blocked style
- Semi-blocked style

Examples of each style, with corresponding elements keyed to each section, are found on pages 88 and 89.

The **fully-blocked style** begins all letter elements, except the heading on pre-printed letterhead, at the left-hand margin. Paragraphs are not indented.

The **square-blocked style** follows the same pattern with the exception that the date, initial and enclosure lines are placed near the right-hand margin. This form has two advantages: it gives the letter more of a balanced look and enables you to get more information on one page.

The **modified-blocked style** further rearranges the elements of the letter by placing the heading, date line, closing, and signature line near the right-hand margin. All other elements begin at the left-hand margin.

The **semi-blocked style** is similar to the modified-blocked style except the paragraphs are indented from five to ten spaces each. This form is one of the most widely used in business.

LAYOUT AND DESIGN

Your letter should look clean, crisp, uncluttered, and professional. You can achieve such a look by paying particular attention to how it is laid out

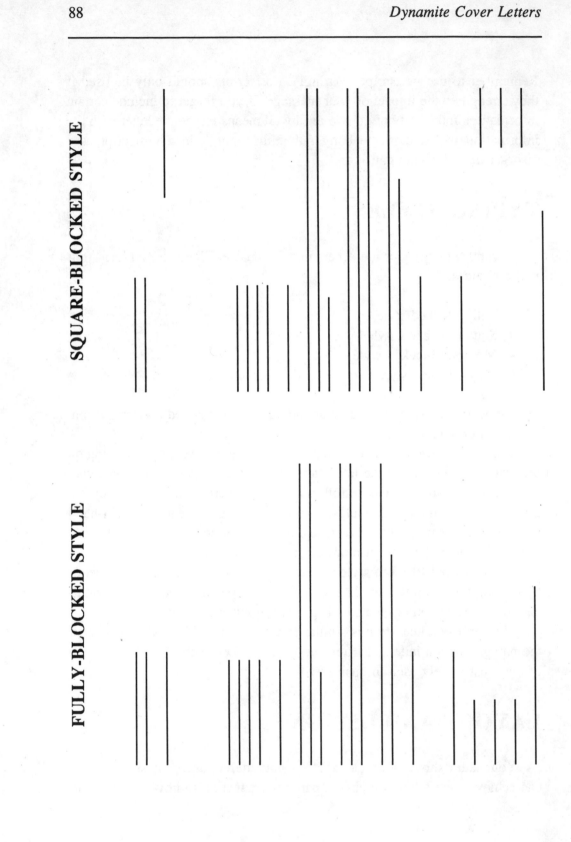

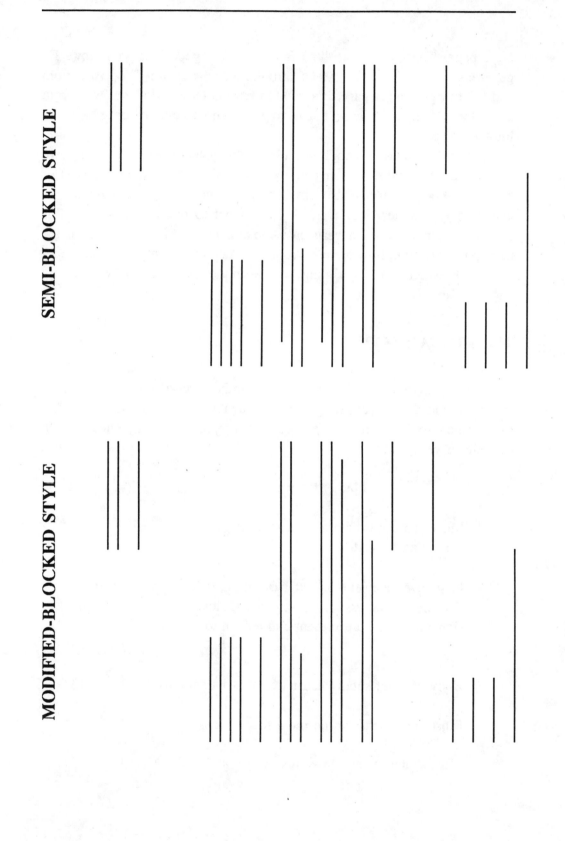

on a page. The cliche that "less is more" is a good rule to follow. Be generous with white space. Make sure the letter is centered top to bottom and left to right on the page. It's good to keep at least a 1¼" to 1½" margin around the page. A 1" margin begins to give letters a cluttered or unbalanced look.

You can emphasize important points in your letter, as well as improve its overall readability, by using various symbols such as bullets (• • •) or boxes (▪ ▪ ▪). You can also emphasize by underlining, capitalizing, or changing type styles. However, be careful not to over-emphasize in this manner and thus create a very busy-looking letter. Many readers dislike having their reading flow broken frequently. You may want to emphasize by using only bullets and underlining, such as in the resume letter examples on pages 70 and 71.

EVALUATION

Once you've completed a letter, examine the quality of its form, structure, and design according to the following evaluation criteria. Circle the numbers to the right that best describe the presence or absence of each element in your letter.

Elements	Yes	No
1. Makes an immediate good impression and is inviting to read.	1	3
2. First seven elements in letter (heading, date line, inside address, salutation, body, closing, signature lines) are present and adhere to the rules.	1	3
3. Body of letter subdivided into 2 to 4 paragraphs.	1	3
4. Most paragraphs run no more than 5 lines.	1	3
5. Most sentences are 25 words or less in length.	1	3

6. Includes complete name and address of
   letter recipient.   1   3

7. Signed name strong and confidently using
   a fountain pen.   1   3

8. Selected a standard typing style.   1   3

9. Has a clean, crisp, uncluttered,
   and professional look.   1   3

10. Used a 1¼" to 1½" margin around
    the top, bottom and sides.   1   3

TOTAL

Add the numbers you circled to get a composite score. If your score comes to "10", your letter demonstrates strong elements of form, structure, and design. Correct any elements that receive a "3" so that your letter will become a perfect "10".

Chapter Five

ORGANIZATION AND CONTENT

Assuming your letter is impressive enough to pass the five to ten second reading test, what you say and how you say it will largely determine if the reader will take desired actions. The power of your paper must move the reader to action. You can best do this by observing the rules of effective letter organization and content.

COMMON MISTAKES

Individuals who receive hundreds of letters from job seekers report similar problems with most letters they read. Letters that don't pass the five to ten second test tend to include several of these errors:

- **Looks unprofessional in form, structure, and design:** Many letters neglect the basic rules of form, structure, and design as outlined in Chapter Four. They look amateurish rather than reflect the professional competence of the writer. They don't demonstrate the writer's best professional effort.

- **Addressed to the wrong person or sent to the wrong place.** Many letter writers still forget to include proper contact information or send their letters to the wrong people and places. Make sure your letter includes a complete return address and a telephone number you can be reached at during the day. Also, closely check the name and address of the person who will receive your letter.

- **Does not relate to the reader's knowledge, interests, work, or needs.** Many letter writers fail to research the needs of their audience and target them accordingly. They simply waste employers' valuable time. If you respond to an ad or vacancy announcement, make sure you address the requirements specified for submitting your letter and resume.

- **Includes spelling, grammatical, and punctuation errors.** The worst mistakes you can make in a letter are spelling, grammatical, or punctuation errors. These are unforgiving errors that clearly communicate your incompetence. Such mistakes demonstrate you are either careless or semi-illiterate—both deadly to a job search!

- **Uses awkward language and the passive voice.** Carefully watch your use of language and try to mainly use the active voice. The active voice gives your writing more energy. Good, crisp, interesting, and pleasing language is something few readers experience in reading letters.

- **Overly aggressive, assertive, boastful, hyped, and obnoxious in tone.** Employers receive many letters from individuals who try to impress them with what is essentially obnoxious language. They think that telling an employer they are the *"hottest thing since sliced bread"* will get them an interview. These letters even appear in some books that claim they are examples of "outstanding letters"! We have yet to encounter employers who are impressed by such letters. They tend to be low class letters that follow the principles of low class advertising.

- **Self-centered rather than job or employer-centered.** Too many job applicants still focus on what they want **from** employers (position, salary, benefits) rather than what they can do **for** employers (be productive, solve problems, contribute to organization, give benefits). Make sure your letters are oriented toward employers' needs. Tell them about the **benefits** you will give them. If you start referring to "you" rather than "I" in your letters, you will force yourself to be more employer-centered.

- **Poorly organized, difficult to follow, or wanders aimlessly.** Many letter writers still fail to plan the logic, sequence, and flow of their letters. They often begin with one idea, wander off to another idea, continue on to yet another disconnected idea, and then end the letter abruptly with no regard for transitions. Readers often must examine the letter two or three times to figure out what the writer wants. Such poor writing is inexcusable. If you can't say something in an organized and coherent manner, don't waste other peoples' time with your drivel!

- **Unclear what they are writing about or what they want.** Is there a goal or purpose to this letter? Many letters still lack a clear purpose or goal. They assume the reader will somehow figure out what they are writing about! Make sure your letter has a clear purpose. This should be revealed in the first paragraph.

- **Says little about the individual's interests, skills, accomplishments, or what they expect to achieve in the future.** Your job search letters should tell letter recipients what it is you can do for them. Unfortunately, many letter writers fail to communicate their strengths and benefits to potential employers.

- **Fails to include adequate contact information.** Be sure to include your complete address, including zip code, and a daytime telephone number. Do not use a P.O. Box number.

- **Dull, boring, and uninspired.** Employers are looking for individuals who have enthusiasm, energy, and fire. However, most letters they receive give little indication of these critical characteristics. Try to use language that expresses your enthusiasm, energy, and fire. At least start with the active voice!

- **Too long.** Busy people don't have time to read long letters. Chances are you can say just as much, and more effectively, in a short letter. Follow the principle of "less is best."

- **Poorly typed.** We still receive letters from people who use a typewriter with dirty keys and worn ribbons. They often make typing errors and then try to correct them with erasures, chalk tape, Liquid Paper, or Wite-Out. The result is an amateurish looking letter that reflects poorly on the professional style and competence of the letter writer. If you write a job search letter, make sure it reflects your **best** professional effort.

- **Produced on cheap and unattractive paper.** Professional correspondence should be produced on good quality paper. However, many letter writers cut corners and go with poor quality paper. Don't be cheap. Good quality paper only costs a few cents more than the cheap product and it's easy to find at your local stationery or print shop.

In other words, many letters are just poorly written; they make poor impressions on readers. Letters that avoid these errors tend to be read and responded to. Make sure your letters are free of such errors!

PRINCIPLES OF GOOD ADVERTISING

Several principles of effective advertising can be adapted to business writing and the job search. Indeed, the advertising analogy is most appropriate for a job search since both deal with how to best communicate benefits to potential buyers and users. These principles should assist you in developing your creative capacity to get what you want through letter writing.

Job search letters should be written according to the key principles of good advertising copy. They should include the following principles:

- **Catch the reader's attention:** While advertising copy primarily captures attention through a visual (headline, photo, illustration), a job search letter can do the same. It should project an overall quality appearance and an opening sentence or paragraph that immediately grabs the reader's attention. Like any good presentation, an attention-grabbing opening can be a question, startling statement, quotation, an example or illustration, humorous anecdote, a suspenseful observation, or a compliment to the reader. You must do this at the very beginning of your letter—not near the end which may never get read or where the reader's attention span has dissipated. You should always present your most important points first.

- **Persuade the reader about you, the product:** Good advertising copy involves the reader in the product by stressing **value and benefits**. It tells why the reader should acquire the product. A good job search letter should do the same—the product is you and the letter should stress the specific benefits the reader will receive for contacting you. The benefits you should offer are your skills and accomplishments as they relate to the reader's present and future needs. Therefore, you must know something about your reader's needs before you can offer the proper mix of appealing benefits.

- **Convince the reader with more evidence:** Good advertising copy presents facts about the product that relate to its benefits. An effective job search letter should also present evidence of the writer's benefits. Statements of specific accomplishments and examples of productivity are the strongest such evidence.

- **Move the reader to take action (acquire the product):** Effective advertising copy concludes with a call to take action to acquire the product. This is usually in the form of a convenient order form or a toll free telephone number. To stress the benefits of the product without moving the reader to take action would be a waste of time and money. When writing job search letters, you should conclude with a call to action. This is the ultimate power of your paper. You want the reader to do something he or she ordinarily would not do—pick up the telephone to contact you, or write you a positive letter that leads to job search information, advice, and referrals as well as job interviews and offers. But we know few letters are so powerful as to move the reader to take initiative in contacting the letter writer. Simply put, the benefits are not as clear in a job search letter as they are in selling a product through advertising copy. Therefore, your call to action should mention that **you** will contact the reader by telephone at a certain time.

Form, style, content, production, and distribution all play important roles in communicating these persuasive elements in your letters.

Your letters should represent <u>you</u>—
your personality, your credibility,
your style, and your purpose.

PLANNING AND ORGANIZING

It goes without saying that you need to plan and organize your writing. By all means do not copy or edit a letter you think may be a good example of an effective job search letter. "Canned" letters tend to be too formal. Worst of all, they look and sound canned and thus they lack credibility.

Your letters should represent **you**—your personality, your credibility, your style, and your purpose. Start by asking yourself these questions **before** organizing and writing your letters:

- What is the **purpose** of this letter?

- What are the **needs** of my audience?

- What is a good opening sentence or paragraph for grabbing the **attention** of my audience?

- How can I maintain the **interest** of my audience?

- How can I best end the letter so that my audience will be **persuaded** to contact me?

- How much **time** should I spend revising and proofreading the letter?

- Will this letter represent my **best professional effort**?

After writing your letter, review these questions again. But this time convert them into a checklist for evaluating the potential effectiveness of your letter:

- Is the **purpose** of this letter clear?

- Does the letter clearly target the **needs** of my audience?

- Does the opening sentence or paragraph grab the **attention** of my audience?

- Does the letter sustain the **interest** of my audience?

- Will the letter **persuade** the reader to contact me?

- Have I spent enough **time** revising and proofreading the letter?

- Does the letter represent my **best professional effort**?

Always keep in mind what you want your audience to do in reference to your job search:

- Pay attention to your message

- Remember you

- Take specific actions you want taken

CONTENT RULES

The body of the letter should clearly communicate your message. How well you structure this section of the letter will largely determine how much impact it will have on your reader.

The basic principles of effective communication are especially applicable to the body of your letter. In general you should

1. **Have a clear purpose in writing your letter:** First ask yourself *"What message do I want to convey to my reader? What do I want him or her to do after reading my letter?"* Your message should be directly related to some desirable action or outcome.

2. **Plan and organize each section:** Each paragraph should be related to your overall purpose as well as to each other. The message should be logical and flow in sequential order. Start with a detailed outline of your message.

3. **Put your most important ideas first:** Since readers' attention decreases in direct relation to the length of a message, always state your most important points first.

4. **Keep your paragraphs short and your sentences simple:** Your reader is most likely a busy person who does not have time to read and interpret long and complex letters. The shorter the letter the better. Plain simple English is always preferred to complex usages which require the reader to re-read and decode your language. Three to four paragraphs, each three to five lines in length, should be sufficient. Keep sentences to no

more than 25 words. Avoid including too many ideas in a single sentence.

5. **Your opening sentence should get the attention of the reader:** Your first sentence is the most important one. It should have a similar function as an advertisement— get the interest and involvement of your audience. Avoid the standard canned openers by making your sentence unique.

6. **Your opening paragraph should clearly communicate your purpose:** Get directly to the point in as short a space as possible. Remember, this is a business letter. Your reader wants to know why he or she should spend time reading your letter. Your first sentence should tell why and begin motivating him or her to take actions you desire.

7. **Your letter should convince the reader to take action:** Most letters function to inform and/or to persuade. In either case, they should lead to some action. Incorporate the four principles of good advertising in your letter writing:

   - Catch the readers attention.
   - Persuade the reader about you or your product— establish your credibility.
   - Convince the reader with more evidence.
   - Move the reader to acquire the service or product.

8. **Follow of rules of good grammar, spelling, and punctuation:** Grammatical, spelling, and punctuation errors communicate a lack of competence and professionalism. Check and re-check for such errors by (1) proofreading the letter yourself at least twice, and (2) asking someone else to proofread it also.

9. **Communicate your unique style:** Try to avoid standard or "canned" business language which is found in numerous how-to books on business writing and sample letters. Such language tends to be too formalistic and boring. Some examples go to

the other extreme in presenting excessively aggressive and obnoxious letters which would turn off any normal employer. Write as if you were talking to a reader in a natural conversational tone. Be honest and straightforward in your message. Use your imagination in making your letter interesting. Put your personality into this letter. Try to demonstrate your energy and enthusiasm through your writing tone. For example, what type of impression does this letter leave on a reader?

> I'm writing in response to your recent ad for an assistant manager at your Great Falls Super store.
>
> Please find enclosed a copy of my resume which outlines my experience in relationship to this position.
>
> Thank you for your consideration.

While this letter is short and to the point, it doesn't grab the reader's attention, sustain his interest, nor move him to action. It screams "b-o-r-i-n-g!" It sounds like hundreds of canned cover letters employers receive each day. Why not try writing with more personality and energy? Consider this alternative:

> Last year I increased profits by 15 percent at Star Drugs. It was a tremendous challenge, but the secret was simple—conduct the company's first management review which resulted in reorganizing the pharmaceutical and video sections. We eliminated two full-time employees and dramatically improved customer service.
>
> I'm now interested in taking on a similar challenge with another company interested in improving its productivity. When I saw your ad in Sunday's <u>Toledo Star</u>, I thought we might share a mutual interest.
>
> If you're interested in learning more about my experience, let's talk soon on how we might work together. I'll call you Thursday afternoon to see if you have any questions. In the meantime, please look over my enclosed resume.

Which letter do you think will grab the attention of the employer and lead to some action? The first letter is both standard and boring. The second letter, equally true, incorporates most principles of effective letter writing—and advertising!

10. **Be personable by referring to "you" more than "I" or "we":** Your letters should communicate that you are other-centered rather than self-centered. You communicate your awareness and concern for the individual by frequently referring to "you".

11. **Try to be positive in what you say:** Avoid negative words and tones in your letters. Such words as "can't", "didn't", "shouldn't", and "won't" can be eliminated in favor of a more positive way of stating a negative. For example, instead of writing

> I don't have the required five years experience nor have I taken the certification test.

Try putting your message in a more positive tone:

> I have several years of experience and will be taking the certification test next month.

12. **Follow the basic ABC's of good writing:** These consist of <u>A</u>lways <u>B</u>eing:

   - Clear
   - Correct
   - Complete
   - Concise
   - Courteous
   - Considerate
   - Creative
   - Cheerful
   - Careful

INCLUSIONS AND OMISSIONS

What should be included and omitted in your cover letters? This question depends on your purpose and your audience. If you are responding to a vacancy announcement or a classified ad, you need to address the stated requirements for submitting an application. This usually involves a resume and sometimes information on your "salary requirements".

Use the following general guidelines when trying to decide what to include or omit in your letters:

THINGS YOU SHOULD INCLUDE:

- Positive information that supports your candidacy.

- Information on your skills, abilities, strengths, accomplishments, interests, and goals.

- Examples of your productivity and performance.

- Benefits you can offer the reader.

- A daytime contact telephone number.

THINGS YOU SHOULD OMIT:

- Any extraneous information unrelated to the position, the employer's needs, or your skills.

- Any negative references to a former employer, your weaknesses, or the employer's organization and position.

- Boastful statements or proposed solutions to employer's problems.

- Salary requirements or history.

- References.

- Personal information such as height, weight, marital status, hobbies—information that also should not appear on a resume.

One major question concerning many job applicants is whether or not to include salary information in their letter. Our general rule is to omit such information in your letter; never volunteer salary information unless asked for it since this is the last question you want to deal with **after** you have demonstrated your value in job interviews. However, it is not always possible to avoid the question. In certain situations you must address the salary question in your letter. But job ads or vacancy announcements, for example, often request a statement about your salary requirements or salary history. If you don't respond, you may be eliminated from consideration. Be careful in how you respond to this requirement. When asked, state a **salary range** rather than a specific salary figure. If, for example, you currently make $40,000 a year but you expect to make $50,000 in your next job, you might state your salary expectation is *"in the range of $48,000 to $54,000."* When stating your salary history, make sure to include your total compensation package—not just your monthly salary figure.

Never, never, never volunteer your weaknesses or negatives.

The basic rule for including information in cover letters is to include only positive information that stresses your skills and abilities in reference to the employer's needs. Never, never, never volunteer your weaknesses or negatives. These are subjects which may be discussed during a job interview, but you should never put them in writing.

The biggest problem facing most job seekers is keeping focused on their goal. The job search is an intensely ego-involved activity that often goes astray due to a combination of wishful thinking and bouts of depression attendant with rejections. If you keep focused on your goals, what you include or omit in your cover letters will come naturally. You will know what should be communicated to employers as your qualifications.

EVALUATION

Evaluate the quality of the organization and content of your letters by responding to the following evaluation criteria. Circle the numbers to the right that best describe your letter.

Characteristic	Yes	No
1. Immediately grabs the reader's attention	1	3
2. Presents most important ideas first.	1	3
3. Expressed concisely.	1	3
4. Relates to the reader's interests and needs.	1	3
5. Persuades the reader to take action.	1	3
6. Free of spelling, grammatical, and punctuation errors.	1	3
7. Incorporates the active voice.	1	3
8. Avoids negative words and tones; uses positive language throughout.	1	3
9. Expresses the "unique you."	1	3
10. Employer-centered rather than self-centered.	1	3
11. Stresses benefits the reader is likely to receive from the letter writer.	1	3

12. Demonstrates a clear purpose.	1	3
13. Sentences and paragraphs flow logically.	1	3
14. Includes complete contact information (no P.O. Box numbers).	1	3
15. Expresses enthusiasm, energy, and fire.	1	3
16. Follows the ABC's of good writing.	1	3

TOTAL

Add the circled numbers to arrive at your composite score. If you incorporate the principles identified in this chapter into the organization and content of your writing, your letter should score a perfect "16".

Chapter Six

QUALITY PRODUCTION

Whatever you do, make sure your letters look **and** feel professional. Remember, most employers review qualifications of strangers. They work with limited information that provides only a few indicators of professional competence.

The production quality of your letters is an important indicator of professional competence to employers. You not only communicate your competence, style, judgment, and class through the form, structure, organization, and content of your letters (Chapter Four and Five), you also communicate these same qualities at the production end. Therefore, you must create the right "look". This involves choosing the proper production equipment, type style and size, and paper quality and color. All such production factors must come together to produce dynamite letters for your successful job search.

PRODUCTION EQUIPMENT

Your letters should always be neatly typed. While handwritten letters will give your job search a personal touch, this is not what you should be striving to achieve at this point in the job search. Handwritten letters are inappropriate when writing to employers. The general rule to follow is this: Employers want to see your best professional efforts. They are unforgiving of your errors. Poor judgment, improper style, and lack of class will be remembered as incompetence. Handwritten letters—including the more personalized thank-you letters—say nothing about your professional competence. They, instead, may say something about your judgment, or lack thereof!

Employers want to see your best professional efforts.

What type of machine produces the most professional looking letters? Without a doubt a wordprocessed letter produced on a laser printer looks best. Assuming you proofread your copy, as well as ran a "spellcheck" program to catch all spelling errors, such machines produce error-free, letter quality products. However, not everyone has access to such equipment. At the very least you should produce your letters on a good quality typewriter. By "good quality" we mean one that gives a neat, clean appearance—no evidence of errors in the forms of strike-overs, erasures, or chalk white-outs. Most electric typewriters with an expert typist behind them produce such a look. If you know you make errors, use a typewriter with correcting-tape capabilities.

If you use a typewriter, be sure to check on the quality of the ribbon and print. Many people still type letters on worn cloth ribbons that produce weak looking type. It is best to use a typewriter with a carbon or film ribbon. If you must use a typewriter with a cloth ribbon, make it a rule to change to a new ribbon as soon as you begin producing your first job search letter and resume. Also, check the keys to make sure they are clean. Typewriter keys do accumulate gum and dirt that leave unsightly marks on paper. If you use an old machine whose keys are out of line, change to one that produces an even line type.

Be sure to double check the copy setting on electric typewriters and printers. Many times print quality is too light or too dark because of incorrect settings. Adjust the setting for one to three copies, depending on what looks the neatest and cleanest.

This is not a good time to begin learning to type. If you can't type, or you consider yourself a poor typist who makes numerous mistakes, find someone to do this work for you. If need be, hire a professional typist to produce your letters. It will be money well spent. But make sure you thoroughly proofread their final product.

If your letters demonstrate your best professional effort, then there are no excuses for typing errors. Be sure you thoroughly proofread the final product. Better still, have someone else also proofread the letter. If you use a wordprocessor, make sure you run a "spellcheck" program in addition to proofreading before printing the letter.

If you use a wordprocesser, make sure you print the letter on a letter quality printer. Many letter writers still use dot matrix printers that print less than 30 dots per character. They further compromise print quality by using worn ribbons—some haven't changed the original cloth ribbon since purchasing the printer! Such products look terrible even though they are produced on ostensibly higher level technology than a typewriter.

If your choices are between a non-letter quality dot matrix printer and a typewriter, go with the typewriter. Such dot matrix printers communicate the wrong message—your letter was probably mass produced similar to junk mail. Dot matrix printers should be used for drafting documents or printing data. They are best used for billing purposes—businesses report their accounts pay quicker when the bills are printed on dox matrix printers, because the assumption is the billing is computer-generated and thus more accurate than bills printed on letter quality machines. Job search letters produced on dot matrix printers communicate a lack of class as well as project a computer-generated, mass mailing image. However, many near letter quality dot matrix printers produce an acceptable look. When in doubt, hold the paper 15 inches from your nose and ask yourself this question: Does this letter look mass produced? If it does, change to a letter quality machine, or step down to a typewriter!

Perhaps the best test for evaluating the professional look of your letter is to find nine of the best looking business letters you have seen over the past year. Put your letter in the pile and then rank the ten according to their professional "look". If your letter doesn't look as good as the top three, start over and produce something more acceptable. Remember, your letter should demonstrate your best professional effort to employers.

TYPE STYLE AND SIZE

The rule for selecting type style is this: go with something conventional that is also easy to read. If an electric typewriter or wordprocessing program and printer give type style choices, select one of the following: Courier, Bookface Academic, Prestige Elite, Times Roman, Palatino, New Century, or ITC Bookman. These are standard type styles appearing in most business letters, newspapers, magazines, and books. Avoid Helvetica, Gothic, Script, or any italicized style. While these are attractive styles for certain types of communication, they are more difficult to read compared to our first choices.

If your wordprocessor permits you to vary type size, select a 10 to 12 point size, depending on the characteristics of the type style. Courier in 10 point, for example, is similar in size to Palatino in 11 point. You will probably want to stay close to 11 point. In some type styles 10 point is too small. In most type styles 12 point begins to look a bit large. For your reference, most of the text in this book is Times Roman style which is sized at 11.5 point.

JUSTIFICATION, HYPHENS, AND PARAGRAPHS

If you use a wordprocessing program, be sure only the left side is justified; the right side should be unjustified or ragged edge. Fully justified letters look too formal. Also, all words along the right-hand side should be complete words—no hyphens should break words. Make sure you double-space between paragraphs.

PAPER CHOICES

The size, quality, and color of your paper also say something about your professional style and competence. You should be conventional once again.

You should always type or print your letter on 8½ x 11 inch paper to fit into either a No. 10 business envelope or a 9 x 12 inch envelope. Smaller paper looks too personal and presents a weak image.

The paper you choose should both look and feel professional. Whatever you do, avoid xerox, onion skin, or erasable papers. These look and feel cheap. For a few dollars you can purchase top quality paper at most stationery, office supply, or print shops. Choose 20 to 50 pound bond paper with a 100% cotton fiber or "rag content". If the paper has a definite texture to it, select one with a fine texture rather than one that looks and feels very coarse or rough. Avoid very thick papers as well as any scented papers.

Darker shades of any color can dull your message.

Conventional paper colors for job search letters are white, off-white, ivory, or light grey. Contrary to what others may advise, basic white stationery is very acceptable today. It presents a clean, crisp look of class that may stand out next to the many off-white and ivory letters that flood today's job market. If you choose to go with light grey paper, keep it very light. Darker shades of any color can dull your message. Unless you are applying for an artistic or creative position, where you are expected to express a unique and unconventional style, avoid other colored papers.

It's best to send your letter in a matching envelope—same paper weight, texture, and color.

PRODUCE A "10" LETTER

Evaluate your final product in reference to the following checklist. Compare your letter according to each evaluation criteria and then rate it by circling the numbers to the right. When you finish, add the numbers circled for an overall cumulative score.

Characteristic	Yes	Maybe	No
1. Has an overall strong professional appearance sufficient to make an immediate favorable impression.	1	2	3
2. Used a new or nearly new ribbon with clean keys or printer head.	1	2	3
3. Adjusted copy setting properly—not too dark, not too light.	1	2	3
4. Type appears neat, clean, and straight.	1	2	3
5. Printed with a standard type style and size.	1	2	3
6. Produced on a letter quality machine.	1	2	3
7. Proofread and/or ran "spellcheck" for possible spelling/typing errors.	1	2	3
8. Used good quality paper stock that both looks and feels professional.	1	2	3
9. Selected a paper color appropriate for my audience.	1	2	3
10. Compared to nine other business letters received over the past year, this is one of the three best in appearance.	1	2	3

TOTAL

If your cumulative score is between 10 and 15, you are on the right track in producing professional looking letters. If your score is higher than 15, go back to the drawing broad. Keep improving the production quality of your letter until it receives a perfect "10"!

Chapter Seven

EFFECTIVE DISTRIBUTION

Distribution also plays an important role in demonstrating your best professional effort. How and to whom you send your letters does make a difference. The method of delivery can elicit an immediate response or no response at all. While we do not recommend engaging in unconventional delivery methods—such as the story of the young man who sent his shoe in a shoebox accompanied by a "powerful" one sentence cover letter saying *"Now that I've got my shoe in the door, how about an interview?"*—you should at least pay attention to the details involved in effectively delivering your letters.

CHOICES

Your distribution choices are numerous. You may decide to shotgun (broadcast) a cover letter and resume to hundreds of "Dear Sir/Madam" employers or selectively target only 10 employers by their correct name and title. You may decide to raise the attention and response level of your letter recipients by using special next-day delivery services or enclose your letter in a brightly printed, attention-getting envelope. Or your may decide to type the letter but handwrite the address as well as affix a nice commemorative stamp to the envelope. While these considerations may initially appear insignificant in comparison to your important message, they can and do make a difference in how quickly and how well your letters are read and responded to.

THE ENVELOPE

In most cases you should send your letter in a matching No. 10 business envelope. However, if your letter is accompanied by a resume or other printed materials, you may want to use a 9 x 12 inch envelope. This large envelope presents your materials better to the recipient. It stands out from other envelopes. More importantly, it means your materials will arrive neat and flat. The receiver need not unfold your letter or struggle to keep it flat should the paper tend to spring back to the folded position.

Try to select an envelope that matches the color, weight, and texture of your letter. However, if you choose a 9 x 12 inch envelope, you may not be able to match it with the stationery. In this case either use a plain white or manila (tan) envelope or select an attention-getting color—red or blue will stand out. Alternatively, you may choose a special pre-printed priority or next-day envelope available at the a U.S. Post Office or through UPS, Federal Express, or a courier service. All of these envelopes stand out from the crowd of No. 10 business envelopes.

We recommend typing the address on the envelope. Some people claim a handwritten address is more personal and thus more powerful. However, it's not as professional as a neatly typed address. Be sure to include your return address in the upper left-hand corner. You should never affix a pressure sensitive mailing label to a No. 10 business envelope. Such labels look like machine affixed addresses and thus immediately downgrade letters to junk mail.

How will you affix the postage? Many people claim it's better to personalize the postage by using a nice commemorative stamp. Others say it's best to affix the postage by postal meter since it looks more professional since this is the standard way businesses affix their postage. This is probably another one of those proverbial *"six one way, half a dozen another"* type of decisions. In the end, it may not make much difference. When in doubt, use postage stamps. A postage meter may give the wrong impression—you are "stealing" postage from your present employer.

Should you decide to broadcast hundreds of letters and resumes to those "Dear Sir/Madam" employers, it really doesn't make much difference how you affix the postage. In fact, since you already decided to make your letter impersonal and you probably won't get many positive responses, you might as well save some money and send them the least expensive way possible.

TO WHOM IT MAY CONCERN

It's always preferable to address your letter to a specific person by name. If you don't, chances are your letter will be thrown away or given little attention. After all, why should someone take you and your job search seriously if you won't take them seriously enough to at least learn their name? If you don't know to whom you should send your letter, you should make a few phone calls to find out. Call the organization and ask the operator or receptionist some version of this question:

> *"Hi, I need some information. I'm sending a letter to the head of the marketing department, but I'm not sure I have the correct name and address. Could you help me?"*

This question will easily get you the correct information. It only takes a phone call and a few seconds of your time. Don't be *"pennywise but pound foolish"* or lazy in literally addressing your letter to no one!

If you decide to broadcast your resume to hundreds of organizations, you obviously have decided to use a junk mail approach to employers. In this case, you probably will not address your letters to a specific name unless you have access to a specialized mailing list that includes the names appropriate to your job search. If you lack names, at least address your letters to a position, such as "Director of Personnel", "Director of Marketing", "Vice-President of Manufacturing", or "Director of Public Affairs". Assuming the mail room does not discard it, your letter should find its way to the proper person. As we noted in a previous chapter, avoid sexist, anonymous, and wimpish salutations such as "Dear Sir", "To Whom It May Concern", or "Gentlepeople". If you know the position, open your letter with the name of the position: "Dear Director" or "Dear Vice-President". You may want to eliminate the salutation altogether. However, don't hold your breath in expectation of receiving an avalanche of responses from such generic letters!

BEST METHODS

What's the best way to send your letters? Most job search letters are sent first-class through the regular mail. However, if you really want to make an impression on an employer and seek an immediate response, send it by special overnight or next-day air services. These services are conveniently available through the U.S. Postal Service, Federal Express, UPS, or other couriers. Such services may cost anywhere from $9.00 to $35. While your mail will probably be signed for in the mail room or by a receptionist, it should be handled separately and delivered quickly to the individual.

While these services may get the recipient's immediate attention, they do not guarantee immediate action nor positive responses. What they do is shorten the time span between when you send the letter and when you speak with the recipient about the letter. You will still need to follow-up with a telephone call. Make sure you call the same day the individual is supposed to receive your letter. Since most of these special services guarantee delivery by 11am, make your telephone call sometime between 2pm and 4pm that same day. When you do call, mention that you sent your letter by special overnight delivery service. The delivery service itself becomes the lead in for your telephone conversation. Introduce yourself by asking if the individual received your letter that morning.

> *"Hi, this is Mary Stafford. I'm calling in reference to a letter I sent you yesterday by Federal Express. Did you receive it this morning? Have you had a chance to read it yet?"*

The individual will most likely remember receiving your letter. If not, chances are he or she will look for it immediately to verify receiving it. With this phone call, you increase the likelihood your letter will get read and responded to. By sending your letter for next day delivery, your letter recipient should be better prepared to discuss your letter—and remember you.

You also can register or certify your letter to get the attention of your letter recipient. However, this service delivers your letter in two to three days, or perhaps longer. If you want to make an impression and get immediate feedback, go with the special overnight delivery services which guarantee a morning delivery.

Never fax your letter or resume unless requested to do so by someone. The poor quality of fax paper and images will not enhance your professional image. If someone requests you to fax your letter and/or resume, make sure you also put your original copies in the mail. Type at the top left side of the letter the date you faxed the information: "Faxed July 9". Also, immediately follow-up your fax with a phone call to make sure the fax was received and to inquire if the individual has any questions or needs any additional information.

> ### *You must be doggedly persistent in writing targeted letters and following-up with phone calls.*

TARGETING

The most effective letters are targeted on specific individuals. They demonstrate some knowledge of the individual and his organization. This knowledge is gained through research on the organization or acquired through referrals received as part of your networking activities. If you demonstrate your knowledge of the individual and the organization, or initiate the letter through a referral and follow-up with a phone call, your letter recipient should be responsive to you. If you make a habit of writing three targeted letters each day, you will begin building a large network of employer contacts that will eventually turn into job interviews and offers. However, you must be doggedly persistent in writing targeted letters and following-up with phone calls.

BROADCASTING

If you choose to broadcast letters and resumes to hundreds of potential employers, be perfectly honest with yourself. This is not the most productive use of your job search time nor money. You're engaging in a junk mail exercise that will be lucky to elicit more than a one percent positive response rate. Many first-time junk mail users have unrealistic expectations of the effectiveness of such strategies. Many questionable employment firms that promote resume and letter writing services tied to customized mailing lists and printing services promote such unrealistic expectations; some charge over $2,000 and produce near scandalous results! Unfortunately, many job seekers still engage in wishful thinking when they resort to this direct mail activity. They are reaching hundreds of employers they would not other reach through targeted letters and telephone calls. They believe their phone will start ringing any day with numerous invitations to interview.

The hard realities of job search junk mail are often these: no responses and a few *"Thank you, we'll keep your resume of file"* or *"Sorry, we have no positions at present for someone with your qualifications"* letters. These responses should not be taken as hopeful signs of an impending job vacancy for which you will be considered. They are merely polite rejections penned by employers who are unwilling to give job applicants all of the bad news—they have thrown your resume and letter away!

FOLLOWING-UP

Writing letters without following-up is a recipe for communication failure. Always think of the processes of writing, producing, and distributing as the first three steps in a four-step letter effectiveness process. Following-up is the critical fourth step which determines whether or not your letter is read and responded to. If you fail to follow-up, you kill your chances of experiencing the fruits of the first three steps.

Always keep in mind that few busy people immediately respond to letters with a letter or phone call. You should never assume someone is neither interested in you nor are they inconsiderate for not responding to your letter. Why should they respond just because you decide to take their time intruding into their daily work routines by writing a letter? If they responded to every letter they receive each day, they would not have time to get any of their work done! Instead, approach this situation from a different assumption altogether. When you send your letter, assume your recipient is a very busy person who will not respond unless you complete the fourth step in the letter effectiveness process. Their response is contingent upon the quality of your follow-up activities. In fact, a typical recipient of a job search letter will quickly read it and then put it aside so they can get back to their more important daily work.

Writing letters without following-up is a recipe for communication failure.

Therefore, if you want a response to your letter, **you** must take the initiative to follow-up with a phone call. Your call will generate a response. In some cases, the individual may not remember receiving your letter and thus requests you to send another copy by mail or fax. Your follow-up activities will quickly educate you on the difficulties inherent in managing job search communications. You will learn most people who receive your letters are very busy people who have difficulty remembering any one letter or resume received on a particular day or week. Busy people have deadlines, priorities, meetings to attend, and decisions to make. Seriously reading unsolicited mail is a luxury few busy people can afford. Regardless of how intrinsically good your letter may be, it still must compete with many other letters each day. In the end, what may make your letter stand out and be remembered amidst the crowd are your follow-up activities. We will examine these activities in the next chapter.

EVALUATING

Examine the potential effectiveness of your letter distribution activities by responding to the following evaluation criteria:

Action	Yes	No
1. Addressed to a specific name.	1	3
2. Used a No. 10 business or a 9 x 12 inch envelope.	1	3
3. Checked to make sure all enclosures got enclosed.	1	3
4. Matched the envelope paper stock and color to the stationery (if No. 10 business envelope).	1	3
5. Typed the address and return address.	1	3
6. Affixed a commemorative stamp.	1	3
7. Used a special delivery service for overnight delivery.	1	3
8. Followed-up letter immediately with a phone call.	1	3

TOTAL

If you answer "no" to any item other than No. 7 or your cumulative score is higher than 8, be sure to make the necessary changes. This is not the time and place to make mistakes that can negatively affect the overall quality of your enclosed letter and accompanying materials.

Chapter Eight

DYNAMITE IMPLEMENTATION AND FOLLOW-UP TECHNIQUES

We've always been fascinated why people read "how-to" job search books but never seem to get their job search on track. Many people find such books "interesting" and "helpful". They may even attend a job search seminar or take a college course on the subject. Some even become book and seminar "junkies"; they repeat the process of reading more job search books and attending more seminars. Some get stuck trying to do a self-assessment, continuously asking themselves *"Who am I?"* and *"Where am I going in life?"* They seem preoccupied with contemplating their future rather than interested in contacting, meeting, and getting feedback from potential employers. Others crank out resumes and cover letters which they send to only five employers. They wait and they wait and they wait. Then they wonder why there seem to be so few jobs available and why no one wants to hire them.

So they read another book and discover they did everything that they were told to do, but nothing seems to happen to them. Maybe the book was bad, or maybe they aren't good. Somehow all this "how-to" advice doesn't seem to work. In the meantime, they engage in a great deal of wishful thinking that somehow the ideal job will come their way if only they read more books and attend more seminars!

Let's be honest with ourselves and all the "how-to"advice you encounter. Good jobs do not come by way of understanding a process nor by way of osmosis. They only come your way if you take the necessary **actions** to bring them within the scope of your job search. You must take certain actions and repeat them over and over again. Those actions must go beyond reading more books and attending more job search seminars. It's time to free yourself of the books and get on with the business of making things happen on a daily basis.

> *You must take certain actions and repeat them over and over again.*

IMPLEMENTATION FOR RESULTS

The basic failure with most job searches is the inability to implement and follow-through. Individuals may learn all the tricks to writing effective letters and resumes as well as how to conduct effective interviews and negotiate salaries. But if they don't translate their **understanding** into concrete and purposeful **repetitive actions**, they will go nowhere with their job search.

The process of translating understanding into action is what we call **implementation**—the ability to make things happen according to plan. At the very heart of implementation is the repetitive process of **follow-up**. Without an effective follow-up campaign focused on all of your job search communications and actions, your job search is likely to founder. You'll become a resident of that never-never land of "no responses" to your letters.

COMMIT YOURSELF IN WRITING

At the very least, implementation requires you to put together an action plan and commit yourself to seeing it become a reality. You may find it useful to commit yourself in writing to implementing your job search. This is a very useful way to get both motivated and directed for action. Start by completing the job search contract on page 124 and keep it near you—in your briefcase or on your desk.

In addition, you should complete weekly performance reports. These reports identify what you actually accomplished rather than what your good intentions tell you to do. Make copies of the performance and planning report form on page 125 and use one each week to track your actual progress and to plan your activities for the next week.

If you fail to meet these written commitments, issue yourself a revised and updated contract. But if you do this three or more times, we strongly suggest you stop kidding yourself about your motivation and commitment to find a job. Start over again, but this time consult a professional career counselor who can provide you with the necessary structure to make progress in finding a job.

A professional may not be cheap, but if paying for help gets you on the right track and results in the job you want, it's money well spent. Don't be *"penny wise but pound foolish"* with your future.

FOLLOW-UP

Follow-up is a much neglected art, but it is the key to unlocking employers' doors and for achieving job search success. But many people fear following-up. Like giving a speech, it requires talking with strangers! They would rather put their letters in the mail and wait for the telephone to ring or for a return letter.

Follow-up occurs at the implementation stage of your job search. It is the single most important element for converting communications into action. Without an effective follow-up campaign, your letters and resumes are likely to lose their impact. They will probably sit on someone's desk amidst numerous other letters and resumes. If you want dynamite job search letters—ones that move readers to actions that eventually lead to job interviews and offers—you must engage in a series of follow-up activities that will give your letters their intended impact.

JOB SEARCH CONTRACT

1. I will begin my job search on _____.
                                      (specific date)

2. I will involve _____ with my job search.
                          (individuals/groups)

3. I will complete my skills identification step by _____.
                                                         (specific date)

4. I will complete my objective statement by _____.

5. I will complete my resume by _____.

6. I will complete my first round of job search letters (approach and cover) by _____.

7. I will begin my networking activities on _____.

8. Each week I will:

   ■ make _____ new job contacts.
   ■ write _____ job search letters.
   ■ conduct _____ informational interviews.
   ■ follow-up on _____ referrals.

9. I expect my first job interview will take place during the week of _____.

10. I expect to begin my new job by _____.

11. I will manage my time so that I can successfully complete my job search and find a high quality job.

    Signature: _____

    Date: _____

WEEKLY JOB SEARCH PERFORMANCE AND PLANNING REPORT

1. The week of: _____.

2. This week I:

   - wrote ____ job search letters.
   - sent ____ resumes and ____ letters to potential employers.
   - completed ____ applications.
   - made ____ job search telephone calls.
   - completed ____ hours of job research.
   - set up ____ appointments for informational interviews.
   - conducted ____ informational interviews.
   - received ____ invitations to a job interview.
   - followed-up on ____ contacts and ____ referrals.

3. Next week I will:

   - write ____ job search letters.
   - send ____ resumes and ____ letters to potential employers.
   - complete ____ applications.
   - make ____ job search telephone calls.
   - complete ____ hours of job research.
   - set up ____ appointments for informational interviews.
   - conduct ____ informational interviews.
   - follow-up on ____ contacts and ____ referrals.

4. Summary of progress this week in reference to my Job Search Contract commitments:

   _____

   _____

   _____

   _____

   _____

HOW TO KILL
A PERFECT LETTER

It only takes seven simple words to kill a job search letter and thereby deaden your job search:

"I look forward to hearing from you."

Even six words will do it: *"Thank you for your consideration."* If you close your letters with these standard statements, you effectively kiss your letter and resume goodbye! You'll be lucky if five percent of your letter recipients will take the initiative to contact you based on these closing statements.

Such statements are the most commonly used closings in job search letters. They are also the most ineffective closings. Consider for a moment what the seven word statement means. What are you saying? Do you want the letter recipient to give you a call? If this is what you mean—and a literal reading of this sentence confirms such an expectation—then you are in for a big disappointment.

It is simply inconsiderate on your part to expect the person to contact you.

Why should a busy person bother writing you—a stranger who is trying to get something out of them—a letter or giving you a telephone call? Just because you expect it or because it's a nice thing to do? Let's get our heads turned on straight and deal with the realities of business communication etiquette. No one owes you a letter or telephone call just because you decided to interrupt their schedule with a job search letter. This statement basically says you really don't care if you ever hear from the reader. Accordingly, you will most likely not hear from the reader. Not that the reader is inconsiderate or not interested in talking with you. It's just that your letter initiative provided no follow-through mechanisms for making the connection other than expecting the reader to call you! It is simply inconsiderate on your part to expect the person to contact you. What should they contact you about? Acknowledge receiving your letter? Share their experience with you? Give you some job leads? Offer you a job? Wish you well? What exactly is it you want the reader to contact you about?

RESCUING YOUR LETTER

It's incumbent upon **you** to take follow-up initiative. The first thing you need to do is to never, never, never end your letter with those six or seven deadly words. Instead, always complete your letter with a **follow-up statement** which calls for **you** to initiate a specific **action** related to the contents of your letter. These statements can come in many different forms:

> I will call your office Tuesday afternoon, July 17, to see if your schedule would permit us to meet briefly.

> I know you're very busy. But I also know I could benefit greatly from your advice. I would like to call you on Wednesday morning to briefly discuss my interests. I'll only take a few minutes of your time.

> I will call your office at 2:30pm on Thursday, July 19, to ask you a few questions about my interests and to see if we might be able to get together for a brief meeting in the near future.

> Would next week be a good time to discuss my interests? I'll call your office at 3pm on Monday, July 16, to check your schedule. I appreciate your time.

Notice that each statement specifies **what** you will do and **when** you will do it—an expected action. The reader now knows what to expect next from you. At this stage he or she needs to do nothing other than **remember** you and your letter—the most important outcome you want to achieve when initially developing a communication link with your reader.

Being remembered is extremely important to an effective job search. Individuals who get remembered are those whose letters get read and who receive referrals. Put yourself in the shoes of the reader. Assume you receive 25 job search letters a day. Twenty-two writers end their letters with the seven deadly words. Three writers close by saying they will call the reader at a specific time to discuss the questions, issues, or interests raised in the letter. Which of the 25 letters are you most likely to remember, especially when you have a calendar facing you on your desk telling you the phone is likely to ring at particular times during the next few days? You will probably re-read the letters from the three individuals who said they would call. You want to determine if it's worth taking the calls. In addition, you want to prepare for each call by acknowledging receipt of the letter and demonstrating your knowledge of its contents. You may also want to ask a few questions. If on re-reading the letter you decide you really don't want to talk to this individual, then you will be prepared to nicely say *"no"* when you take the call or you will give this message to one of your staff members who will nicely tell the caller that you really don't have time, you can't help them, and you wish them *"good luck"*.

In either case, as the letter writer your follow-up actions lead to desirable outcomes. If you are able to talk directly with the individual, you will most likely acquire useful information. If you get a rejection, you at least know you need not waste anymore time with this potential contact. Go on to other more promising job search connections.

EFFECTIVE FOLLOW-UP OPTIONS

You have basically two follow-up options. You can write another letter requesting a response to your first letter or you can telephone the person. Writing another letter merely attempts to force the reader to take the initiative in contacting you—not our idea of a bright follow-up activity. You're merely moving more paper on to the individual's already crowded desk. Your first follow-up letter will most likely not generate the intended response. However, your fourth or fifth follow-up letter will probably be acknowledged. At this point you have sufficiently pestered the person into action. Pestered people tend to respond in two different ways:

- They feel guilty for not having responded to you earlier and thus are very willing to discharge this professional obligation by spending some time on the phone talking with you and giving you useful information.

- They feel put upon by strangers who have no business expecting them to take valuable time to respond to the writer's "personal" matters. They write a short letter acknowledging your communications and telling you they can't help or aren't interested in further contacts with you.

However, pestering people and putting them on guilt trips is no way to conduct an effective job search.

Your second follow-up option is a telephone call. This is our preferred follow-up method. It's both efficient and effective. But keep in mind two important characteristics of a follow-up telephone call:

- It is probably your first verbal contact with the individual after having communicated via the written word and paper. As such, this call may become your first **interview** even though you are only attempting to ask a few questions or set up an appointment. Be prepared to conduct an interview as soon as you make this follow-up call. The individual may not want to see you, but would be happy to answer any questions you have over the telephone. This means being prepared with specific questions, knowing how to answer questions, and projecting yourself properly over the telephone. You should have a pleasing telephone voice and sound coherent (complete sentences, no repetitious *"uhs"* or *"ya know"* or high-pitched voices). Keep in mind what's happening is this telephone encounter: your letter recipient is now associating a voice with your written materials. What you say and how you say it may determine if the individual wants to also see your face by scheduling a face-to-face interview!

- Telephone follow-ups can be very frustrating. You will be lucky to directly contact the person on your first, second, or even third phone call. The person may be out of the office, attending an important meeting, or avoiding you altogether. In some cases it may take eight phone calls before you can speak directly with the person! In other cases you may never get to talk to the person—only receive a message through a gatekeeper.

MULTIPLE FOLLOW-UPS

Conducting an effective follow-up is easier said than done. A typical follow-up may require three to seven phone calls because the person is unavailable or avoiding your call. With each phone call you may need to leave a message. However, similar to response rates to letters, don't expect busy people to return phone calls from strangers. Many people only do so after the third or fourth redundant phone message—guilt moves them to action!

A typical follow-up may require three to seven phone calls.

Whatever you do, please do not show your irritation, anger, or disappointment in not having your phone calls returned. Some people feel insulted and express their irritation in their tone of voice or choice of words when they make their third, fourth, or fifth ineffective follow-up call:

> *"Well, I left two messages—one on Tuesday and another on Wednesday."*

> *"Does he usually return his phone calls?"*

> *"What should I do? I keep calling but he won't return my calls!"*

> *"Did he leave a message for me?"*

> *"How many more days should I wait before I call again?"*

These responses communicate the wrong attitude toward someone who may be able to assist you. While they may accurately reflect what's happening, they lack tack and good job search manners. Keep your cool and cheerfully keep leaving messages as if you understand this is what normally happens in the course of conducting follow-up calls.

A standard follow-up scenario goes something like this. You stated in your letter you would call at 2:30pm on Tuesday. When you call you will probably have to go through one or two gatekeepers before you can make direct contact with the person you want to reach. The final gatekeeper will probably be a personal secretary or receptionist who is well versed on the art of screening important from not-so-important calls. When the final gatekeeper takes your call, the following exchange is likely to occur:

SECRETARY: *"Mr. Carroll's office. How can I help you?"*

YOU: *"Hi, this is Mary Harris calling for Mr. Carroll."*

SECRETARY: *"I'm sorry, Mr. Carroll is not available."*

YOU: *"When would you expect him to be free?"*

SECRETARY: *"I really don't know. He's been in meetings all day. Could I take a message and have him return your call?"*

YOU: *"Yes, would you please? My name is Mary Harris and my telephone number is _____. I'm calling in reference to a letter I sent Mr. Carroll on July 5. I mentioned I would be calling him today."*

SECRETARY: *"I'll give him the message."*

YOU: *"Thanks so much for your help."*

Don't hold your breath in expectation of getting a return call soon. The secretary will give him the message, but he probably will sit on it and do nothing until he's motivated to do so. Consequently, you will probably need to initiate another call. If you don't hear from the person within 24 hours, make another follow-up call. This time your conversation may go something like this:

> **SECRETARY:** *"Mr. Carroll's office. How can I help you?"*
>
> **YOU:** *"Hi, this is Mary Harris calling for Mr. Carroll."*
>
> **SECRETARY:** *"I'm sorry, Mr. Carroll is not available. Can I take a message?"*
>
> **YOU:** *"Yes. Can you tell him Mary Harris called. My telephone number is _____. I'm calling in reference to my letter of July 5. I also called yesterday and left a message."*
>
> **SECRETARY:** *"Oh, yes. I remember your call. I did give him the message. However, he's been extremely busy. I'll make sure he gets the message again."*

You may get a return call, but don't hold your breath. You will probably need to initiate another call or two before you make direct contact. Again, wait 24 hours to call again. With a third call you will most likely have the attention of both the secretary and the letter recipient. Both may start to feel somewhat guilty for not taking your call. The secretary especially feels responsible because she obviously has been ineffective vis-a-vis both you and her boss. The letter recipient is beginning to collect a pile of messages indicating the same person is waiting for a return call. At this point the secretary is likely to make certain decisions: the next time you call she will make a special effort to remind her boss that you have called several times, and it would be nice to return the call or give a more hopeful response than *"I'll give him the message"*; or she will ask her boss if she should relay any special message to Mary Harris should she call again. Your fourth follow-up call will usually result in a change in dialogue with the secretary:

SECRETARY:	*"Mr. Carroll's office. How can I help you?"*
YOU:	*"Hi, this is Mary Harris calling for Mr. Carroll."*
SECRETARY:	*"Yes, I remember you called earlier. I'm sorry Mr. Carroll hasn't been able to get back with you. He's been so busy these past few days. When I spoke with him yesterday, he said he would call you today around 4pm."*

Making several follow-up phone calls demonstrates your persistence. While it's unfortunate you may have to make so many follow-up calls, especially if they are expensive long-distance calls, that's the reality of communicating in today's business world. Such persistence pays off because you become remembered and because individuals feel guilty about not returning your calls after receiving the same message over and over again from the same person.

Such persistence pays off because you become remembered and because individuals feel guilty about not returning your calls.

FOLLOW-UP YOUR FOLLOW-UP

Once you make telephone contact, be sure to follow-up this follow-up call with a nice thank-you letter. Again, your goal is not just to get useful job information. Your goal should also include being **remembered** for future reference. You want busy people to remember you because they are likely to refer you to other busy people who may be looking for individuals with your qualifications. In other words, the thank-you follow-up letter becomes an important building block for expanding your network for information, advice, and referrals. Job seekers who follow-up their follow-up calls with a thank-you letter are more likely to be remembered that those who merely hang up the phone and move on to other follow-up calls.

FOLLOW-UP MEANS FOLLOWING-UP

It's funny what you learn about people through their letters. Today more and more job seekers close their letters with an effective follow-up statement, but they never follow-up. They simply don't do what they say they will! Indeed, the last three letters we received from job seekers included the date and time they would call us to follow-up. They wrote nice letters—modeled after the advice of "how-to" job search letter books—but we have yet to hear from them. Somewhere along the way to the mailbox no one told them they actually had to follow-up their letter! Yes, we remember these people, but unfortunately we remember them for what they did to us—wasted our time with a canned follow-up statement they had no intentions of doing anything about.

You simply can't do more damage to your job search than failing to follow-up according to expectations. Many people say they will call on Thursday afternoon, but they never call. It's as if the action follow-up statement has become a routine and meaningless closing for job search letters. Many job seekers merely go through the motions of putting in a "canned" closing statement. Indeed, one wonders how much else in the letter is "canned" or "creatively plagiarized" from examples of "outstanding" cover letters.

Whatever you do, make sure your letters represent **you**. Moreover, make sure you **do** exactly what you say you will do. If you tell your reader you will call them at 2:30 on Thursday afternoon, make sure you call exactly at that time. The person may have penciled-in this time on their calendar to speak with you. If you fail to do so, the individual is likely to remember you in negative terms—this job seeker doesn't follow-through or make appointments! You simply can't recover from such an initial negative impression. You will be wasting both your time and the time of the reader.

EVALUATE YOUR FOLLOW-UP COMPETENCIES

Let's evaluate the potential effectiveness of your follow-up activities. Respond to each of the following statements by indicating how you dealt with each follow-up action:

Follow-Up Actions	**Yes**	**No**
1. Completed the "Job Search Contract".	1	3
2. Completed my first "Weekly Job Search Performance and Planning Report."	1	3
3. Ended my letter with an action statement indicating I would contact the individual by phone within the next week.	1	3
4. Made the first follow-up call at the time and date indicated in my letter.	1	3
5. Followed-up with additional phone calls until I was able to speak directly with the person or received the requested information.	1	3
6. Maintained a positive and professional attitude during each follow-up activity. Was pleasantly persistent and tactful during all follow-up calls. Never indicated I was irritated, insulted, or disappointed in not having my phone calls returned.	1	3
7. Followed-up the follow-up by sending a thank-you letter genuinely expressing my appreciation for the person's time and information.	1	3

Add the numbers you circled to the right of each statement to get a cumulative score. If your score is higher than "7", you need to work on improving your follow-up competence. Go back and institute the necessary changes in your follow-up behavior so your next letter will be a perfect "7"!

Chapter Nine

EVALUATE YOUR EFFECTIVENESS

Evaluation should play a central role in all of your job search activities. If you want to be most effective, you must continuously evaluate your progress throughout each step of your job search. Evaluation based upon specific performance criteria eliminates a great deal of wishful thinking that can confuse and misdirect your job search. Best of all, evaluation helps keep your job search **focused on goals and productive activities** that eventually lead to job interviews and offers.

Be sure to conduct two types of evaluations related to your letters. The first is an **internal evaluation**. This is a self-evaluation you conduct yourself by examining your actions in reference to specific performance criteria. Questionnaires appear at the end of Chapters Four, Five, Six, Seven, and Eight for evaluating how to best structure, organize, produce, distribute, and follow-up your letters.

The second type of evaluation may be more important than the internal evaluation. This is an **external evaluation** which is conducted by someone other than yourself. You ask individuals whose judgment you respect to give you feedback on your job search actions. In the case of letters, you want to find two or three individuals who will read your letters and then give you frank feedback on your writing strengths and weaknesses. This external evaluation is the closest you will get to receiving realistic feedback from the actual letter recipient.

INTERNAL EVALUATION

Once you complete your first job search letter, conduct a thorough internal evaluation based upon the following criteria. Several of these criteria already appeared in previous chapters. They relate to each step in the letter writing process—structure, organization, production, distribution, and follow-up. Respond to each statement by circling the appropriate number to the right that most accurately describes your letter.

Audience	**Yes**	**Maybe**	**No**
1. I know the needs of my audience based upon my research of both the organization and the individual.	1	2	3
2. My letter clearly reflects an understanding of the needs of the organization and the letter recipient.	1	2	3
3. The letter recipient will remember me favorably based on the unique style and content of my letter.	1	2	3
4. My letter offers a benefit to the the reader.	1	2	3

Form, Structure, and Design

	Yes	**Maybe**	**No**
5. Makes an immediate good impression and is inviting to read.	1	2	3
6. First seven elements in letter (heading, date line, inside address, salutation, body, closing, signature lines) are present and adhere to the rules.	1	2	3

7. Body of letter is subdivided into 2 to
   4 paragraphs.   1   2   3

8. Most paragraphs run no more than 5 lines.   1   2   3

9. Most sentences are 25 words or less
   in length.   1   2   3

10. Includes complete name and address of
    letter recipient.   1   2   3

11. Signed name strong and confidently
    using with a fountain pen.   1   2   3

12. Selected a standard typing style.   1   2   3

13. Has a clean, crisp, uncluttered,
    and professional look.   1   2   3

14. Used a 1¼ to 1½ inch margin around
    the top, bottom and sides.   1   2   3

15. Confined to a single page.   1   2   3

Organization and Content

16. Immediately grabs the reader's attention   1   2   3

17. Presents most important ideas first.   1   2   3

18. Expressed concisely.   1   2   3

19. Relates to the reader's interests
    and needs.   1   2   3

20. Persuades the reader to take action.   1   2   3

21. Free of spelling, grammatical, and
    punctuation errors.   1   2   3

22. Incorporates the active voice.	1	2	3
23. Avoids negative words and tones; uses positive language throughout.	1	2	3
24. Expresses the "unique you."	1	2	3
25. Employer-centered rather than self-centered.	1	2	3
26. Stresses benefits the reader is likely to receive from the letter writer.	1	2	3
27. Demonstrates a clear purpose.	1	2	3
28. Sentences and paragraphs flow logically.	1	2	3
29. Includes complete contact information (no P.O. Box numbers).	1	2	3
30. Expresses enthusiasm, energy, and fire.	1	2	3
31. Follows the ABC's of good writing.	1	2	3

Production Quality

32. Has an overall strong professional appearance sufficient to make an immediate favorable impression.	1	2	3
33. Used a new or nearly new ribbon (if cloth) with clean keys or printer head.	1	2	3
34. Adjusted copy setting properly—not too dark, not too light.	1	2	3
35. Type appears neat, clean, and straight.	1	2	3
36. Printed with a standard type style and size.	1	2	3

37. Produced on a letter quality machine.   1   2   3

38. Proofread and ran "spellcheck" (if
    using a wordprocessing program) for
    possible spelling/typing errors.   1   2   3

39. Used good quality paper stock that both
    looks and feels professional.   1   2   3

40. Selected a paper color appropriate
    for my audience.   1   2   3

41. Compared to nine other business letters
    received over the past year, this is
    one of three best in appearance.   1   2   3

Distribution

42. Addressed to a specific name.   1   2   3

43. Used a No. 10 business or a 9 x 12
    inch envelope.   1   2   3

44. Checked to make sure all enclosures
    got enclosed.   1   2   3

45. Matched the envelope paper stock and
    color to the stationery.   1   2   3

46. Typed the address and return address.   1   2   3

47. Affixed a commemorative stamp.   1   2   3

48. Used a special delivery service for
    overnight delivery.   1   2   3

49. Followed-up letter immediately with
    a phone call.   1   2   3

Follow-Up Actions

50. Completed the "Job Search Contract".   1   2   3

51. Completed my first "Weekly Job Search
    Performance and Planning Report."   1   2   3

52. Ended my letter with an action statement
    indicating I would contact the individual
    by phone within the next week.   1   2   3

53. Made the first follow-up call at the
    time and date indicated in my letter.   1   2   3

54. Followed-up with additional phone calls until
    I was able to speak directly with the person
    or received the requested information.   1   2   3

55. Maintained a positive and professional
    attitude during each follow-up activity.
    Was pleasantly persistent and tactful
    during all follow-up calls. Never indicated
    I was irritated, insulted, or disappointed
    in not having my phone calls returned.   1   2   3

56. Followed-up the follow-up by sending a
    thank-you letter genuinely expressing my
    appreciation for the person's time and
    information.   1   2   3

                                            ───────────────

TOTAL

Add the numbers you circled to the right of each statement to get a cumulative score. If your score is higher than 60, you need to work on improving your letter effectiveness. Go back and institute the necessary changes to create a dynamite letter.

EXTERNAL EVALUATION

You can best conduct an external evaluation of your letters by circulating them to two or more individuals. Choose people whose opinions are objective, frank, and thoughtful. Do not select friends and relatives who usually flatter you with positive comments. Professional acquaintances or people you don't know personally but whom you admire may be good evaluators. An ideal evaluator has experience in hiring people in your area of job interest. In addition to sharing their experience with you, they may refer you to other individuals who would be interested in your qualifications. If you choose such individuals to critique both your letter and resume, ask them for their frank reaction—not what they would politely say to a candidate sending these materials. You want them to role play with you—a potential interview candidate. Ask your evaluators:

- How would you react to this letter if you received it from a candidate? Does it grab your attention and interest you enough to talk with me?

- If you were writing this letter, what changes would you make? Any additions, deletions, or modifications?

You should receive good cooperation and advice by approaching people for this external evaluation. In addition, you will probably get valuable unsolicited advice on other job search matters, such as job leads, job market information, and employment strategies.

In contrast to the closed and deductive nature of the internal evaluation, the external evaluation should be open-ended and inductive. Let your reader give you as much information as possible on the quality and potential impact of your letter. Taken together, the internal and external evaluations should complement each other by providing you with maximum information for further strengthening your letter and creating truly dynamite job search letters!

INDEX

CAREER RESOURCES

Call or write IMPACT PUBLICATIONS to receive a free copy of their latest comprehensive, illustrated, and annotated catalog of over 1,000 career resources (books, videos, audiocassettes, computer software).

The following career resources are available directly from Impact Publications. Complete the following form or list the titles, include postage (see formula at the end), enclose payment, and send your order to:

IMPACT PUBLICATIONS
4580 Sunshine Court
Woodbridge, VA 22192
Tel. 703/361-7300
FAX 703/335-9486

Orders from individuals must be prepaid by check, moneyorder, Visa or MasterCard number. We accept telephone and FAX orders with a Visa or MasterCard number.

Qty.	Titles	Price	TOTAL

LETTERS, RESUMES, AND NETWORKING

Qty.	Titles	Price	TOTAL
___	200 Letters for Job Hunters	$14.95	_____
___	Dynamite Cover Letters	$9.95	_____
___	Dynamite Resumes	$9.95	_____
___	Great Connections: Small Talk & Networking for Businesspeople	$11.95	_____
___	High Impact Resumes and Letters	$12.95	_____
___	Instant Job Winning Letters System (IBM software)	$59.95	_____
___	Network Your Way to Job and Career Success	$11.95	_____
___	Perfect Cover Letter	$9.95	_____
___	Perfect Resume	$10.95	_____
___	Perfect Resume Computer Kit (IBM software)	$49.95	_____
___	Resume Catalog	$13.95	_____

JOB SEARCH STRATEGIES AND TACTICS

Qty.	Titles	Price	TOTAL
___	Careering and Re-Careering for the 1990s	$13.95	_____
___	Complete Job Search Handbook	$12.95	_____
___	Discover the Right Job For You	$11.95	_____
___	What Color Is Your Parachute?	$11.95	_____

ALTERNATIVE JOBS, CAREERS, AND EMPLOYERS

Qty.	Titles	Price	TOTAL
___	101 Careers	$12.95	_____
___	American Almanac of Jobs and Salaries	$15.95	_____
___	Best Jobs for the 1990s and Into the 20th Century	$12.95	_____

____ Dictionary of Occupational Titles	$32.95	____
____ Directory of Executive Recruiters (annual)	$39.95	____
____ Educator's Guide to Alternative Jobs and Careers	$13.95	____
____ Encyclopedia of Careers and Vocational Guidance	129.95	____
____ Jobs for People Who Love Travel	$12.95	____
____ Jobs Rated Almanac	$14.95	____
____ New Emerging Careers	$14.95	____
____ Occupational Outlook Handbook (biannual)	$16.95	____

INTERVIEWS AND SALARY NEGOTIATIONS

____ Dynamite Answers to Interview Questions	$9.95	____
____ How to Get Interviews From Job Ads	$16.95	____
____ Interview for Success	$11.95	____
____ Knock 'Em Dead With Great Answers to Interview Questions	$19.95	____
____ Salary Success	$11.95	____
____ Sweaty Palms	$8.95	____

DRESS, APPEARANCE, AND IMAGE

____ Dress for Success	$10.95	____
____ Dressing Smart	$19.95	____
____ Professional Image	$10.95	____
____ Women's Dress for Success	$8.95	____

PUBLIC-ORIENTED CAREERS

____ Almanac of American Government Jobs and Careers	$14.95	____
____ Compleat Guide to Finding Jobs in Government	$14.95	____
____ Complete Guide to Public Employment	$15.95	____
____ Find a Federal Job Fast!	$9.95	____
____ How to Get a Federal Job	$15.00	____
____ Jobs and Careers With Nonprofit Organizations	$13.95	____

INTERNATIONAL AND OVERSEAS JOBS

____ Almanac of International Jobs and Careers	$14.95	____
____ Careers in International Affairs	$15.95	____
____ Complete Guide to International Jobs and Careers	$13.95	____
____ How to Get a Job in Europe	$15.95	____
____ International Jobs	$12.95	____

SUBTOTAL ____

Virginia residents add
4½% sales tax ____

POSTAGE/HANDLING
($3.00 for first title and $.50 $3.00
for each additional book)

____

TOTAL ENCLOSED ------------ ____